BIBLE PROPHECY AND YOU

BIBLE PROPHECY AND YOU

*Predictions, Fulfillments
and What to Watch for Next*

Len Woods

BARBOUR BOOKS
An Imprint of Barbour Publishing, Inc.

Published by Barbour Books, an imprint of Barbour Publishing, Inc., 1810 Barbour Drive, Uhrichsville, Ohio 44683, www.barbourbooks.com

Our mission is to inspire the world with the life-changing message of the Bible.

 Member of the
Evangelical Christian
Publishers Association

Printed in China.

Contents

Part One: Prophecies Fulfilled

Part Two: Prophecies Pending

Conclusion: While We Wait . . .

Appendix:

Chapter 1:

PROPHECY 101

While you read this sentence, millions of people around the world are also wondering about the future.

* Thousands are talking to self-proclaimed psychics on the phone or having their palms read by fortune-tellers while countless others are reading horoscopes online.
* Patrons in a Chinese restaurant, at a table dusted with fortune cookie crumbs, are laughing over a slip of paper that reads, "You will soon meet a mysterious, attractive stranger."
* A group of college students is huddled in a messy dorm room watching *Doctor Who* and imagining what it would be like to travel into the future.

✳ Coworkers in an office break room are discussing the predictions of Nostradamus.

✳ The editorial staff of a supermarket tabloid is busily planning its next big issue: "101 Wild Prophecies and Predictions!"

We humans are fascinated—often obsessed—by the future. We want desperately to know what's ahead.

The bad news? A lot of charlatans who don't know the future are getting rich by convincing a gullible public that they do know the future. The good news? We already have a book that accurately reveals what's to come. That book? The Bible.

THE BIBLE

The Bible is often misunderstood. Many people think it's one book, but it is a collection of sixty-six books. And contrary to what many imagine, the Bible isn't just a rule book—though it definitely contains sections of religious laws. In truth, the Bible is more like a storybook that tells of God's up-and-down relationship with people: how He created the world, how the human race turned away from God and plunged the world into evil and sorrow, what God has done in Christ to

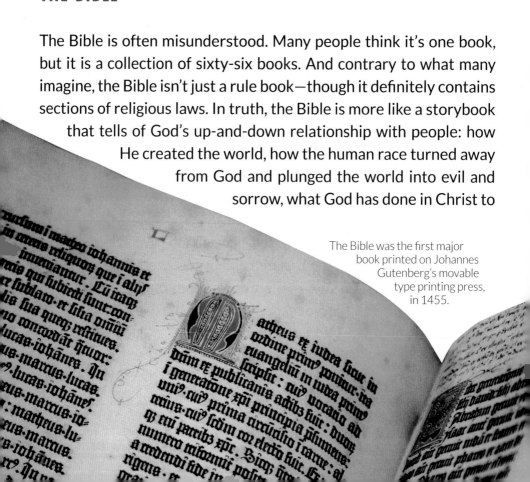

The Bible was the first major book printed on Johannes Gutenberg's movable type printing press, in 1455.

rescue His rebellious but beloved creatures, how God has called His people to live, and what He will eventually do to restore all things.

Many people also malign the Bible, for all sorts of reasons. Some claim we shouldn't trust it, asserting that the so-called Good Book isn't actually good, or that it's just fables written by men who wanted power, or that it's outdated or barbaric or contradictory. The purpose of this book isn't to address all those criticisms. Instead, the goal is to see the Bible through a fascinating set of lenses.

We will look at the many ancient Bible prophecies that have already come true in history. In light of those, we want to wrestle with some questions:

* If the Bible has a perfect record in predicting so many ancient things, should skeptics rethink its trustworthiness in relation to prophecies that have not yet been fulfilled?
* When wondering about the future, should we rely on the scriptures instead of psychics?
* Does the Bible really give us a peek at the future of the world?

Major Old Testament prophets are portrayed in a fresco from a Slovakian church.

THE BIBLE'S EMPHASIS ON PROPHECY

Many people are shocked to discover that about one-fourth of the Bible is considered prophecy. Of the thirty-nine books in the Old Testament, the final seventeen are prophetic in nature. Of the twenty-seven books in the New Testament, the final one, the book of Revelation, is categorized as prophecy. It is widely considered to be the most famous work of prophetic writing in human history.

Even the other forty-eight biblical books—often classified as Historical Books, Wisdom Literature, Gospels, or Epistles—are filled with prophetic passages.

WHAT EXACTLY IS PROPHECY?

Our English word *prophecy* and related words, like the noun *prophet* and the verb *prophesy*, come from a set of extrabiblical Greek words that mean simply "to announce or proclaim." In the Bible, a prophecy is a message from God that is proclaimed (either spoken or written) by a prophet who has been prompted or inspired by God.

Modern preachers like Billy Graham, shown here in 2005, fulfill one aspect of prophecy: *forth*telling. Many biblical prophets were known for *fore*telling—explaining what would happen in the future.

The Old Testament prophet Micah preaches in a
nineteenth-century woodcut by Gustave Doré.

This announcement of God's truth happens in two primary ways: foretelling and forthtelling. Foretelling is what most people think of when they hear the word *prophecy* or *prophet*. Foretelling is the supernatural act of "announcing something in advance." This is the predictive side of prophecy. It's like a good movie trailer—giving you a tantalizing glimpse of a great, exciting story to come. By revealing His will and plans in advance to a prophet, and then by having that prophet deliver His message, God expects His people to respond. The recipients of this divine announcement are expected to adjust to God's purposes by repenting, trusting, obeying, watching, and waiting.

Forthtelling is the present aspect to prophecy. This is where a prophet speaks forth God's Word (or announces God's will in a forth-right manner). Forthtelling holds up divine truth like a mirror and asks, "Does your life look like this? And if not, why not?" When people don't measure up, forthtelling calls for repentance, a change of heart that results in a change of direction.

We see an example of Old Testament forthtelling when the prophet Amos rebukes his countrymen. "This is what the Lord says: . . . They trample on the heads of the poor . . . and deny justice to the oppressed" (2:6–7). We see an example of Old Testament foretelling when Amos relays the rest of God's message: "Now then, I will crush you" (2:13).

To summarize, the essence of biblical prophecy is divine truth— truth about life now and in the future. It's a simple proclamation: This is what God says (a) about how you need to be living *now* (and what will happen if you don't) and (b) about *other things yet to come.*

WHAT DO WE MEAN BY THE TITLE *PROPHET*?

A prophet, simply put, is someone called by God to be His spokesperson or mouthpiece. In ancient times, this calling was symbolized by anointing the designated person with oil.

The Bible shows both men and women fulfilling this prophetic role. Prophets often seemed to have a solitary existence. But the Old

WHAT'S THE SIGNIFICANCE OF ANOINTING?

How did the custom of anointing with oil arise? We know that shepherds sometimes poured oil over the heads of their flocks to keep away pests. The oil made it less likely for bugs to burrow into a sheep's nose or ears. Over time anointing came to signify protection and blessing and enablement.

Throughout the Bible we see prophets, priests, and kings anointed with oil as a sign of God's call on their lives (Exodus 29:7; 2 Kings 9:6). In the Old Testament, the word for *anointed* or *anointed one* is *mashiach*, which is transliterated into English as *messiah*. The New Testament title Christ comes from the Greek *christos*, which also means "anointed." Christians see the baptism of Jesus—in which the Spirit of God descended on Him like a dove (Matthew 3:13–17)—as God anointing Him for His ministry. This is how the writers of the Gospels pointed to Jesus as the ultimate Anointed One—the perfect prophet, priest, and king sent by God for the purpose of bringing salvation to the world.

White House press secretary Sarah Sanders illustrates one aspect of the term *prophet*: one who speaks on another's behalf, in this case, the US president.

Testament also speaks of groups of prophets (1 Samuel 10:5-10) and "the company of the prophets" (1 Kings 20:35; 2 Kings 2:3-7, 15; 4:38; 5:22). At different times, these servants of God apparently lived together in community (2 Kings 6:1-4).

Prophets revealed future events, and they proclaimed God's expectations for people in the present. They chastised rebellious listeners, called them to repent, and warned them of judgment if they did not turn back to God. In addition, prophets heartened discouraged people by reminding them of God's character (His faithfulness, grace, mercy, love, power, etc.). They also comforted those who experienced hopelessness by assuring them of the trustworthiness of God's promises.

It's worth noting that prophets were the original social justice warriors. They spoke up for the poor and the powerless (Isaiah 1:17; Zechariah 7:9-10). They also played an important teaching role and served as sources of wisdom. Although they ministered to the masses, they were also called by God to anoint Israel's kings (1 Samuel

Civil rights activist Martin Luther King Jr., in his famous "Letter from a Birmingham Jail," paraphrased the Old Testament prophet Amos when he said, "Let justice roll down like waters and righteousness like a mighty stream" (Amos 5:24).

10:1; 16:1) and to "speak truth to power" by reprimanding leaders who disregarded God's law (see 2 Samuel 12:7–12).

Most of the biblical prophets were from Israel and Judah, but there were exceptions, such as Balaam in Numbers 22. Usually they spoke to an Israelite audience, but not always; Jonah was called by God to prophesy to the Assyrians in Nineveh.

WHAT ARE THE MARKS OF A TRUE PROPHET OF GOD?

The biblical record speaks of legitimate prophets of God and warns repeatedly of false prophets. How is anyone supposed to know the difference? Simple. The measuring stick is truth. Genuine prophets of God are accurate 100 percent of the time. They tell the truth, no matter what, even when it costs them their lives.

Moses put it this way: "If what a prophet proclaims in the name of the LORD does not take place or come true, that is a message the LORD has not spoken. That prophet has spoken presumptuously, so do not be alarmed" (Deuteronomy 18:22).

False prophets have always managed to find an audience. This is because they speak attractive lies rather than hard truth. They are often slick, gifted communicators. Again, the issue is truth. Moses said that when a so-called prophet's words don't come to pass, we know that both the message and the messenger are illegitimate. In another place, Moses told his fellow Israelites that a false prophet will urge others to stop following the one true God and to pursue false gods (see Deuteronomy 13:1–3).

To summarize, true prophets speak only in the name of the one true God. Their message never encourages evil or condones sin. It will always be consistent with—not contradictory to—the rest of the Word of God. True prophets will constantly confront sin and urge sinners to change their ways. Because of this, those with true prophetic callings were (and still are) extremely unpopular and often persecuted (see 1 Kings 22:26–28; Luke 11:47–54).

A "sorcerer and false prophet named Bar-Jesus" is struck blind by the apostle Paul for resisting the true gospel message in Paphos, Cyprus (Acts 13:4–12).

WHAT'S THE DIFFERENCE BETWEEN A PROPHET AND A SEER?

The biblical writers often called prophets by different titles. The main Hebrew word translated as *prophet* in our English Bibles is *navi*. It comes from the Akkadian root *nabu*, which means "to speak" or "to proclaim." As previously stated, the idea is that a biblical prophet is primarily a spokesperson—one who speaks for God or proclaims divine truth. We see this term first in Genesis 20:7, where it is used of the Jewish patriarch Abraham.

In addition to using the title *prophet*, the Bible speaks of seers. One Hebrew word translated as *seer* is *ro'eh*, which simply means "to see." A seer is literally one who receives divine messages by seeing, perhaps through a vision (see 2 Kings 17:13; Isaiah 29:10; Micah 3:6–7). Samuel, one of the first great prophets in the Bible, was called a seer (1 Samuel 9:9, 11). So was Zadok, who served God as a priest during the reign of David (2 Samuel 15:27). Another Hebrew word translated as *seer* is *hozeh* (from the verb *hazah*, which also means "to see"). The prophets Gad (2 Samuel 24:11) and Amos (Amos 7:12) were described by this word.

SURREXIT ELIAS
PROPHETA QUASI
IGNIS ET VERBUM
IPSIUS QUASI FACULA
ARDEBAT (ECCLI XLVIII,1)

وقام إيليا النبي كالنار وتوقدكلامه
كالشعل (سي ٤٨، ١)

וַיָּקָם אֵלִיָּהוּ הַנָּבִיא כָּאֵשׁ
וּדְבָרוֹ כְּלַפִּיד בֹּעֵר

Elijah was an important prophet who did not write down his messages. This statue, near Israel's Mount Carmel, depicts him slaying a prophet of Baal (see 1 Kings 18:16–40).

THOSE UNPOPULAR PROPHETS

Has there ever been a tougher job description than that of biblical prophet? God called these brave souls to take cryptic or blunt messages (usually some version of "Repent . . . or else!") to hardheaded, hardhearted people. In fact, He told the prophet Jeremiah upfront, "When you tell them all this, they will not listen to you" (Jeremiah 7:27).

Not surprisingly, when the prophets did exactly as they were told, the results were often anything but good. For their efforts, they often were ignored, mocked, roughed up, or martyred (or some combination thereof).

Tradition says that the prophet Amos was brutally murdered and that Jeremiah was stoned to death after having been beaten, put in stocks (Jeremiah 20:1–2), and thrown into a muddy cistern (Jeremiah 38:6). Many scholars think that Isaiah was sawn in two. The Bible explicitly says that Uriah was killed by the sword (Jeremiah 26:20–23) and that Zechariah, the son of Jehoiada, was executed by stoning (2 Chronicles 24:21). In the New Testament, King Herod, angry over the way John the Baptist called him out for engaging in an illicit affair with his sister-in-law, had the prophet imprisoned and then beheaded (Mark 6:24–27). The most famous prophet of all, Jesus, was crucified.

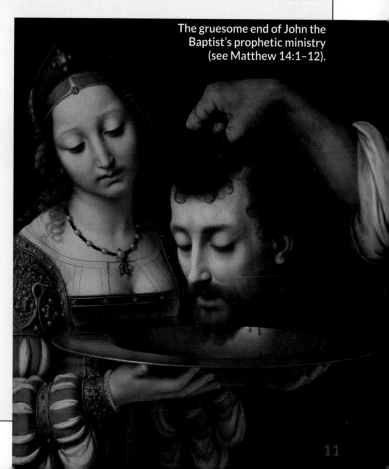

The gruesome end of John the Baptist's prophetic ministry (see Matthew 14:1–12).

Sometimes a prophet was simply labeled a "man of God" (*ish elohim* in Hebrew). Moses (1 Chronicles 23:14), Samuel (1 Samuel 9:6–10), Shemaiah (1 Kings 12:22–24), Elijah (1 Kings 17:18, 24), and Elisha (2 Kings 4:7–9) were all given this title.

Prophets were also called "messengers" (Isaiah 44:26; Haggai 1:13) and "watchmen" (Jeremiah 6:17; Hosea 9:8).

HOW CAN WE CLASSIFY THE DIFFERENT TYPES OF PROPHETS?

The Bible mentions some prophets (Enoch, Elijah, and Elisha, for example) who delivered verbal messages to certain groups of people but did not write down their prophecies for posterity. Other prophets apparently spoke their messages and also committed them to writing. We don't know why God had some but not all prophets preserve their messages. We simply know that the prophecies found in scripture were inspired by God (2 Timothy 3:16).

The Bible's writing prophets served God from the eighth century BC (Hosea and Amos being among the first) until the fifth century BC (Malachi being the last prophet of the Old Testament).

The writing prophets are subdivided into major and minor prophets. (Note: these descriptors have to do with the length of their respective prophecies, not their importance.) The Major Prophets consist of the first five books of prophecy in the Old Testament:

Amos, a shepherd from Tekoa, had a divine vision about the northern Israelite kingdom "two years before the earthquake, when Uzziah was king of Judah and Jeroboam son of Jehoash was king of Israel" (Amos 1:1).

The prophet Joel described a coming "day of the LORD" when "the earth shakes, the heavens tremble, the sun and moon are darkened, and the stars no longer shine" (Joel 2:1, 10).

Isaiah, Jeremiah, Lamentations, Ezekiel, and Daniel. The Minor Prophets are the final twelve books (and the last twelve prophets) of the Old Testament. They are, in order: Hosea, Joel, Amos, Obadiah, Jonah, Micah, Nahum, Habakkuk, Zephaniah, Haggai, Zechariah, and Malachi. The writing prophets can also be grouped into four historical categories.

PROPHETS OF ISRAEL	PROPHETS OF JUDAH	EXILIC PROPHETS	POSTEXILIC PROPHETS
Jonah	Obadiah	Jeremiah	Haggai
Hosea	Joel	Ezekiel	Zechariah
Amos	Isaiah	Daniel	Malachi
	Micah		
	Nahum		
	Zephaniah		
	Habakkuk		

[For an explanation of the terms *exilic* and *postexilic*, see the section "Experiencing Exile" on page 42.]

SUMMARY OF THE MESSAGES OF BIBLICAL PROPHETS

✳ **Jonah** reluctantly preached a message of repentance to the pagan residents of the capital city of Assyria.

✳ **Hosea** vividly illustrated Israel's unfaithfulness to God (by marrying an adulterous woman) and warned the nation to come back to God.

✳ **Amos** appealed bluntly to the wayward people of Israel (the ten northernmost tribes) to return to the Lord.

✳ **Obadiah** foretold the doom of Edom (a neighboring nation).

✳ **Joel** warned the southern kingdom of Judah of imminent judgment if they did not repent.

✳ **Isaiah** implored his people to return to God and be saved, to fix their hope on the coming Messiah, and to resist the temptation to form partnerships with Egypt or Assyria.

✳ **Micah** put the nation "on trial" before God and warned of coming judgment.

✳ **Nahum** pronounced judgment on Assyria about 125 years after Jonah's "revival."

✳ **Zephaniah** declared a mixed message of approaching judgment and future restoration.

✳ **Habakkuk** lamented the lawlessness and injustice of Judah, and he declared that God would use Babylon to punish His people.

✳ **Jeremiah** foretold Jerusalem's coming destruction. Lamentations is his dirge over the fall of Jerusalem and reads like a tear-stained journal.

✳ **Ezekiel** spoke of coming captivity, judgment on the nations, and restoration at the end of the age.

✳ **Daniel** assured his fellow exiles that God has a future for Israel.

✳ **Haggai** urged the Jewish exiles back in the land to finish rebuilding the temple.

✳ **Zechariah** shared visions and oracles with the returned exiles in order to give them hope.

✳ **Malachi** wrote the last book of the Old Testament around 400 BC, predicting the coming of John the Baptist.

WHAT DID THE PROPHETS TALK ABOUT?

The more you read the Old Testament prophets, the more you start
to notice five heavily emphasized topics.

1. **The Law:** The writing prophets constantly hammered at the
    idea that obeying the Law of Moses would lead to blessing and
    that disobeying it would lead to judgment (Leviticus 26:1–39;
    Deuteronomy 28–30).
2. **Repentance:** Again and again the prophets urged the people of
    God to turn from sin and back to God and His law (Isaiah 44:22;
    Joel 2:12).
3. **Exile and restoration:** The prophets assured the people of two
    truths: (1) A failure to repent would ultimately lead to exile
    (removal from the land); and (2) after being exiled for a time,
    they would return to their land (Jeremiah 29:11–14; Ezekiel
    39:25–29).
4. **The Abrahamic covenant.** God's promises to Abraham (Gene-
    sis 12:1–3) were frequently highlighted as a reason for hope.
5. **The coming day of the Lord.** The prophets saw a future day in
    which God would deal ultimately and finally with the wicked—
    and also vindicate the righteous (Amos 5:20; Obadiah 15).

    Other elements of the prophets' messages:

    ❋ Championing the cause of the poor and the oppressed
       (1 Samuel 12:3–4)
    ❋ Condemning the syncretistic tendencies of God's people—
       that is, their habit of mixing pagan elements with worship of
       the one true God (see Jeremiah 7:31)
    ❋ Highlighting God's compassion, mercy, and faithfulness to
       His character (Lamentations 3:22–23; Hosea 11:8)

✳ Bringing hope to downcast people by proclaiming that all was not lost, that God would bring redemption not only for Israel but also for all humankind (Isaiah 9:2–4)

That's a quick summary of the messages of the prophets. What about their methods?

HOW DID THE PROPHETS CARRY OUT THEIR MINISTRIES?

The biblical prophets were fascinating for at least two reasons: their cryptic words and their odd deeds.

CRYPTIC WORDS

You've probably heard the word *oracle*. It's defined as "a person through whom a deity is believed to speak" and can also refer to a divine message relayed to listeners. Worshipers in the ancient Near East often visited pagan temples in hopes of receiving a message from the gods

Ezekiel is famous for both his odd behaviors and strange visions. This stained glass church window from Brussels, Belgium, depicts his vision of four-faced living creatures accompanied by flying wheels. (Read the entire vision in Ezekiel 1:1–28.)

Jeremiah, often called the "weeping prophet," laments the fall of Jerusalem in a seventeenth-century painting by the Dutch master Rembrandt.

through an oracle—usually a priest or priestess believed to have the gift of channeling such communiqués. The Old Testament also uses the word *oracle*. The Hebrew word is *massa'*, which means "burden" or "load." This is fitting, considering the heaviness of many prophetic announcements.

Sometimes prophets spoke in the form of a lament (a "sad song" or "poem") (Isaiah 14:4–21). A lamentation is basically a funeral dirge sung by mourners. Ezekiel, when called to be a prophet, was told by God to eat a scroll full of lamentations (Ezekiel 2:8–10). For this reason, he was full of lament. Ezekiel 27 is a lament for the destruction of the city of Tyre. Ezekiel 32 laments the downfall of Pharaoh and Egypt.

The prophets often spoke in parables. Jesus was the master of parables, communicating difficult ideas through simple stories from everyday life. Parables are ingenious because they offer various layers of understanding. They hide truth from those not yet ready or willing to hear it. One listener may comprehend a superficial but helpful insight, while a more spiritually mature individual might grasp a deeper spiritual truth. A hard-hearted person, however, might think the parable is a waste of everyone's time.

ANCIENT-FUTURE SPEECH

A common feature in prophetic literature is something called *proleptic speech,* a way of describing future events as if they had already occurred. For example, in Psalm 2:6, God says, "I have installed my king on Zion," rather than "I will install my king on Zion." Though this statement refers to a future event, it's written in the past tense. This makes a little more sense when we remember that God is outside of time and is not bound by it. The eternal timelessness of God is difficult to capture using our limited verb tenses.

Prophets commonly used first-person speech. Since God often spoke directly through the prophets—"This is what God the LORD says" (Isaiah 42:5) or "The word of the LORD came to me, saying" (Jeremiah 1:4)—we often see the pronouns *I, me, my,* and *mine* in their pronouncements, either indicating that God is speaking or letting us know that the prophet is speaking for God (Isaiah 45:5; Jeremiah 1:4-5; Malachi 3:6-7). Prophets also employed rhetorical questions to emphasize certain points (Isaiah 49:15; Jeremiah 18:14) and satire (humor, irony, or exaggeration) to make negative points (Isaiah 40:18-20; Jeremiah 46:11).

ODD DEEDS

Prophets sometimes let their actions do all or most of the talking—that is, they'd give bizarre object lessons in public. These shocking behaviors, certain to get attention, are sometimes referred to as sign acts. Through such acted-out parables, the prophets

The prophet Ezekiel has a wild look in this fresco from a Croatian church.

would announce God's message, usually in a provocative way, in order to get the people's attention.

As mentioned earlier, Hosea was told by God to marry a promiscuous, adulterous wife (Hosea 1:2–3). Isaiah was commanded to walk around naked and barefoot for three years (Isaiah 20:2–4). Jeremiah was instructed to take a linen belt he'd been wearing and bury it under some rocks. Later he was told to dig up the rotten garment (Jeremiah 13:1–11). On another occasion he was commanded to put a yoke around his neck (Jeremiah 27).

Ezekiel had to lie on his side for 430 days to symbolize Israel's 430 years of sinfulness (Ezekiel 4:4–8). God told him to cook his food over human excrement (Ezekiel 4:12)! Another time he had to shave his face and head with a sword and divide the hair into three piles; he had to set fire to the first third, walk about the city with the second clump of hair and whack at it with the sword, and scatter the third pile in the wind (Ezekiel 5:1–4).

Imagine how odd and disturbing these actions must have appeared to onlookers. Obviously God knew a great truth of human nature: some people learn best by seeing, not by merely listening.

As we get started, it's not enough to know what biblical prophecy is and how the ancient prophets carried out their God-given roles. The million-dollar question is, *How do we correctly understand the things the biblical prophets have written?*

HOW CAN WE ACCURATELY INTERPRET BIBLICAL PROPHECY?

Imagine the outcome if five detectives and three forensic scientists descended on a crime scene and each decided to follow a unique, personal set of rules for evidence collection and analysis. They'd probably end up with eight different ideas about what the evidence means.

Sadly, interpreting the Bible often becomes a crazy free-for-all like that. It doesn't have to be. There is a science of Bible interpretation called *hermeneutics.* In trying to understand the meaning of cryptic prophetic passages, scholars try to adhere to certain procedures and agreed-upon rules.

1. **Observing lexical and grammatical clues:** Before asking "What does this text *mean*?" they first ask, "What does this text *say*?" They examine the passage, ideally in its original language. Old Testament passages were written in Hebrew or Aramaic, and the New Testament was written in Greek. Scholars look carefully at each word's meaning and how it is used in connection to the other words—in other words, grammar and syntax.

Many of us have watched crime-scene reconstructions on television, as investigators carefully sift through clues to determine the truth of an event. The interpretation of biblical prophecy follows similar methods.

2. **Considering the literary context:** Scholars know it's dangerous to pull a passage out of its context. Verses or prophecies must be viewed in light of the chapter and book in which they're found. Also, the type of literature must be considered.

3. **Examining the historical context:** Knowing the unique setting and circumstances in which an author wrote is indispensable for correctly understanding scripture. Ignoring a passage's historical context can lead to confusion over the meaning of certain words or ideas and, ultimately, to wrong interpretation.

4. **Insisting on theological consistency:** It's critical to remember that the meaning of any one Bible prophecy can't contradict themes, promises, or divine declarations communicated

elsewhere in scripture. Difficult passages must always be interpreted in light of other, clearer passages.

5. **Interpreting scripture in the clearest, most straightforward way (unless there's an obvious reason to do otherwise):** As a general rule, it's wisest and best to take a passage at face value, unless strong evidence calls for a figurative or symbolic interpretation. For example, when Jesus said He was "the vine" (John 15), He was obviously not speaking literally.

6. **Remembering that prophetic literature often conveys time in different ways:** Sometimes prophecies offer fuller descriptions of shorter events than longer ones. Or they skip over large gaps in the prophetic timeline (a device called *telescoping*). Or they don't always list prophetic events chronologically.

7. **Asking good questions:** Did the prophecy pertain exclusively to events in the author's day? Was the prophecy ever fulfilled in Israel's history? Is it speaking of a future event? Could the prophecy have more than one fulfillment?

THE VARIOUS KINDS OF BIBLE PROPHECIES

We can divide biblical prophecies into three groups: (1) those that are historical in nature—given and fulfilled in the past; (2) those that are messianic in nature—related to the life or ministry of Christ; and (3) those that are eschatological in nature—related to the final events of human history.

Thus, we can divide the biblical prophecies into two groups: those that have been fulfilled and those awaiting fulfillment.

It's also important to point out that some prophecies are dual in nature; they include both a short-term and a long-term fulfillment. An example is 2 Samuel 7:12–16. This passage predicts a coming king who would be a descendant of David, build a temple, have an eternal kingdom, and be punished for wrongdoing. In the short-term, Solomon partially fulfilled this prophecy as David's royal heir (1 Kings 2:12), as the builder of the temple (1 Kings 5–6), and as a wayward king (1 Kings 11). But this prophecy also points to the future Messiah whose throne would "be established forever" (2 Samuel 7:16; see Revelation 22:16).

The overall goal of biblical interpretation is to answer a big question: What was the *author's* intended meaning? What *we* want a prophecy to mean, or what we think will best fit our preconceived understanding, is irrelevant.

Even with these excellent rules and scholarly guidelines, the careful study of prophecy can result in many diverse interpretations. This is because Bible readers don't always agree on which passages should be interpreted in a literal way and which ones should be interpreted symbolically or figuratively (guideline number 5).

Rather than portray only one particular school of biblical interpretation, this book will present various interpretive views as we examine the historical, messianic, and eschatological prophecies.

A blueprint for figuring out what prophecies mean is helpful. But there is still a need to substantiate biblical prophecies (especially those that the Old Testament writers say were fulfilled centuries earlier). Without evidence, an Old Testament writer's claim that a prophesied event happened exactly as predicted doesn't always satisfy skeptics. Is there any hard proof that these historic prophecies came to pass? In other words, is this book worth your time?

In the beginning of his novel **The Adventures of Huckleberry Finn**, American author Mark Twain (actual name, Samuel Clemens) posted a notice that reads in part, "Persons attempting to find a motive in this narrative will be prosecuted." Twain's tongue-in-cheek warning does not apply to biblical prophecy.

CAN WE TRUST BIBLICAL PROPHECY?

There is a significant and growing body of archaeological evidence that confirms the fulfillment of many ancient biblical prophecies. These findings argue strongly that we can trust biblical prophecy claims.

Ezekiel, for example, wrote the following prophecy about the ancient coastal city of Tyre (a Phoenician stronghold): "They will destroy the walls of Tyre and pull down her towers; I will scrape away her rubble and make her a bare rock. Out in the sea she will become a place to spread fishnets, for I have spoken, declares the Sovereign LORD" (Ezekiel 26:4–5). Archaeological explorations have confirmed this prediction in detail. The ancient city included a nearby island. When Alexander the Great besieged and destroyed the city in 332 BC, he used the debris from the city to create a land bridge "in the sea" from the mainland to the island.

What about the biblical prophecy foretelling the doom of the Edomites, who, according to Jeremiah, lived "in the clefts of the rocks" (Jeremiah 49:15–18), a location considered impregnable? In 1812, while exploring the towering, rocky desert cliffs about 115 miles southwest of Amman, Jordan (in the region the Bible calls Edom), a Swiss man by the name Johann Burckhardt stumbled upon the ruins of the ancient city of Petra. This well-preserved site is evidence that Jeremiah's prophecy was fulfilled.

These are just two examples of archaeological evidence that substantiates biblical prophecy.

Petra, Jordan, now a popular tourist site, provides evidence
of the trustworthiness of biblical prophecy.

So far we've covered definitions, explanations, and ground rules.
Why so much introduction and setup? To study any complex topic, it
helps to have the big picture. One last question will help us round out
that panoramic view before we start looking at the biblical prophecies that have already been fulfilled.

ARE THERE ANY BENEFITS FROM STUDYING BIBLE PROPHECY?

Studying Bible prophecy benefits us in the following ways:

Strengthens our overall confidence in the Bible. Maybe you are not sure about the Bible. If so, our hope is that this book will enlighten and encourage you. Seeing how so many events foretold in the Bible long ago have come to pass exactly as predicted shows us that the Bible is worthy of our time—and our trust.

Helps us understand God's "long pauses." From the end of the New Testament until now, there has been a gap of more than nineteen centuries. It would be easy to conclude from this fact that maybe God isn't going to make good on all His unfulfilled promises. It would also be wrong. Consider that four centuries passed from the end of the Old Testament to the beginning of the New Testament. So, it took a long time for ancient

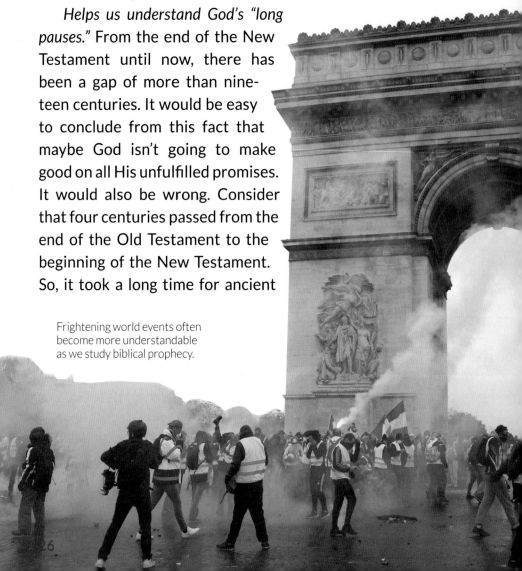

Frightening world events often become more understandable as we study biblical prophecy.

prophecies about the Messiah's first advent to be fulfilled. But they did eventually come to pass. We can see that God was (and always is) at work—even when it doesn't seem like He is.

Helps us understand the times we live in. We face many of the same issues today that the people in biblical times faced—injustice, racial animosity, materialism, greed, immorality, and spiritual apathy. The prophets' warnings can steer us in different, better directions. Their reminders and assurances can help us in very practical ways.

Keeps us from becoming fearful. The more we see that God is in control of our world and that history really is *His story*, the less fear we have of the future. God is moving all creation toward a certain end. Jesus fulfilled numerous prophecies at His first coming. When He comes again, He will fulfill the prophecies that are yet unfulfilled. Instead of fretting, we can look forward to a new heaven and a new earth, where there will be no tears or sorrows or death or pain.

Equips us to identify false prophets and recognize evil. Those who are oblivious to the many biblical predictions about how false messages will flourish and how evil will spread in the last days are at risk of being duped and destroyed.

Readies us for the return of Christ. The New Testament writers repeatedly instructed believers to "keep watch" and stay awake (Matthew 25:13; Ephesians 5:14; 1 Thessalonians 5:5–6). They also encourage us to be holy and to persevere. As the apostle James wrote, "You too, be patient and stand firm, because the Lord's coming is near" (James 5:8). Awareness of what's ahead motivates us to prayerfully engage in gospel conversations with our neighbors and coworkers.

If you still aren't sure there are benefits from studying prophecy, consider that the last book of the Bible begins with this startling promise: "Blessed is the one who reads aloud the words of this prophecy, and blessed are those who hear it and take to heart what is written in it, because the time is near" (Revelation 1:3).

Now it's time to look at some Bible prophecies. Let's begin with some prophecies about the nation God established so that He might pour out His blessings on the world.

Revelation 11:15 says that an angel's trumpet blast will announce the time when "the kingdom of the world has become the kingdom of our Lord and of his Messiah."

Part One:

PROPHECIES FULFILLED

Chapter 2:

PROPHECIES CONCERNING ISRAEL

In the first eleven chapters of the Bible, it's almost as if the author—believed by most conservative scholars to be Moses—is surveying the world through a wide-angle lens. His emphasis is on big sweeping realities: creation (Genesis 1–2), the fall of humans into sin and death (Genesis 3–5), the great flood of divine judgment (Genesis 6–9), and the beginning of nations (Genesis 10–11).

Then, in Genesis 12, it's as if the writer puts a telephoto lens on his camera and zooms in on one elderly, childless couple. Then the rest of the Pentateuch (the five books of Moses—Genesis, Exodus, Leviticus, Numbers, and Deuteronomy) and the other books of the Old

Testament proceed to tell the hard-to-believe story of how God gave this couple a child and expanded the family into twelve large tribes, ultimately forming them into the nation we know as Israel. The point of this epic story is that, at just the right time, God would bring blessing and salvation to the whole world through a prophesied Messiah.

As we follow this story, we notice all along the way God making promises to His chosen people regarding their future—and also making good on those promises.

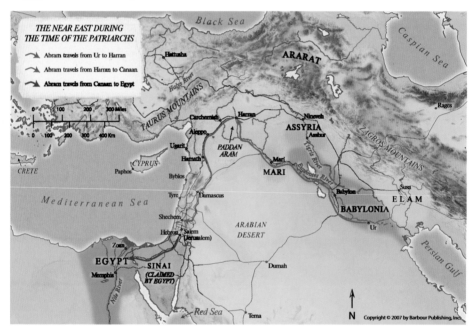

To understand the biblical prophecies concerning Israel, we have to look at God's dealings with the aforementioned couple. The man's name was Abram—later changed to Abraham. He was married to Sarai—better known to us as Sarah. They lived in Ur, near the Persian Gulf.

One day the Lord—that is, the one true God of the Bible, not one of the pagan deities of the ancient Near East—spoke these words to Abram:

"Go from your country, your people and your father's household to the land I will show you. I will make you into a great nation, and I will bless you; I will make your name great, and you will be a blessing. I will bless those who bless you, and whoever curses you I will curse; and all peoples on earth will be blessed through you." (Genesis 12:1–3)

Abram, who was seventy-five at the time, obeyed without hesitation. He packed up his sixty-five-year-old wife and all their earthly belongings and followed God to the land of Canaan. Once he got there, "the LORD appeared to Abram and said, 'To your offspring I will give this land'" (Genesis 12:7).

In just a few verses, Genesis 12 gives us a concise outline for how the Jewish nation fits into biblical prophecy. God's promises? Abraham would become a nation, be blessed, and become great. His descendants would inherit Canaan. They would be a blessing to all nations, and yet they would be cursed by some.

Let's look briefly at each of those broad predictions and how they came to pass.

At God's invitation, Abraham looks at the night sky. God promised to make Abraham's descendants as numerous as the stars (Genesis 15:5).

BECOMING A NATION

It's easy to understand why Abraham's eyes might have widened at hearing God say, "I will make you into a great nation" (Genesis 12:1). He and Sarah had long-term fertility issues (Genesis 11:30). Not only this, but he was seventy-five (Genesis 12:4) and she was sixty-five (see Genesis 17:17). At their ages, they were more likely candidates for a nursing home, not for building a nursery *in their home*.

When ten years passed without any morning sickness or baby bumps, the couple figured that maybe God's plan was to provide children through a surrogate. So, at Sarah's request, Abraham impregnated Hagar, Sarah's maidservant. She delivered a son named

Ishmael. At age eighty-six, Abraham was finally a father!

For thirteen years Abraham assumed that Ishmael must be step one of God's plan to make him into a great nation. But when Abraham was ninety-nine, God appeared to him (Genesis 17:1) and made it clear that He still planned to give Abraham a son—to be named Isaac—by his wife, Sarah (17:16, 19). Sure enough, "the LORD was gracious to Sarah as he had said, and the LORD did for Sarah what he had promised. Sarah became pregnant and bore a son to Abraham in his old age, at the very time God had promised him" (Genesis 21:1–2).

ABRAHAM'S GREAT NAME

One of God's promises to Abraham was, "I will make your name great." Who would deny that Abraham is one of the most famous figures in all of human history? He's mentioned almost three hundred times by name in the Bible, and he's revered not only by Jews and Christians but also by Muslims.

Isaac grew up, married, and had fraternal, very different twin sons: Esau and Jacob. Esau became the father of the Edomites. Jacob—later known as Israel—became the father of twelve sons and a daughter. From this family tree, the twelve tribes of Israel came into existence. Following the exodus from Egypt and their covenant with God at Mount Sinai (see the book of Exodus), the Hebrew people were at last a nation—just as God had promised.

It's hard to believe that God had once taken the elderly, childless Abraham outside on a cloudless night and said, "Look up at the sky and count the stars—if indeed you can count them. . . . So shall your offspring be" (Genesis 15:5). It's wild to think that God had once promised to make a scoundrel like Jacob "prosper" and make his descendants "like the sand of the sea, which cannot be counted" (Genesis 32:12).

But He did.

An angel stops Abraham from sacrificing the son who would fulfill God's promise to turn Abraham into a great nation. God was testing Abraham, who passed—and his family line would continue through young Isaac (see Genesis 22:1–18).

INHERITING THE PROMISED LAND

God's promise of land to Abraham and his descendants (Genesis 12:7) is a primary point of emphasis for the Old Testament writers.

Just in case Abraham misunderstood or wasn't paying attention, God soon repeated this promise of land: "The LORD said to Abram ... 'Look around from where you are, to the north and south, to the east and west. All the land that you see I will give to you and your offspring forever. I will make your offspring like the dust of the earth, so that if

anyone could count the dust, then your offspring could be counted. Go, walk through the length and breadth of the land, for I am giving it to you'" (Genesis 13:14–17).

Genesis 15 records a solemn ceremony, during which God said it again: "To your descendants I give this land, from the Wadi of Egypt to the great river, the Euphrates—the land of the Kenites, Kenizzites, Kadmonites, Hittites, Perizzites, Rephaites, Amorites, Canaanites, Girgashites and Jebusites" (Genesis 15:18–21).

Not long after this, He reiterated the promise to Abraham: "The whole land of Canaan, where you now reside as a foreigner, I will give as an everlasting possession to you and your descendants after you; and I will be their God" (Genesis 17:8). In Genesis 22, He repeated the promises again.

In Genesis 26:2–6, the Lord told Abraham's son Isaac what He had said to Abraham:

> The LORD appeared to Isaac and said, "Do not go down to Egypt; live in the land where I tell you to live. Stay in this land for a while, and I will be with you and will bless you. For to you and your descendants I will give all these lands and will confirm the oath I swore to your father Abraham. I will make your descendants as

Modern Hebron, in the West Bank. Abraham built an altar to God at Hebron, shortly after God had promised him "all the land" that he saw (Genesis 13:14–17).

numerous as the stars in the sky and will give them all these lands, and through your offspring all nations on earth will be blessed, because Abraham obeyed me and did everything I required of him, keeping my commands, my decrees and my instructions." So Isaac stayed in Gerar.

Isaac's son Jacob later had a similar conversation with God in which the Almighty offered a similar assurance. "

"I am the LORD, the God of your father Abraham and the God of Isaac. I will give you and your descendants the land on which you are lying. Your descendants will be like the dust of the earth, and you will spread out to the west and to the east, to the north and to the south. All peoples on earth will be blessed through you and your offspring. I am with you and will watch

PROPHETS TO THE KINGS

During the period when Israel was a united kingdom, roughly 1050–930 BC, and even after the nation split into northern and southern kingdoms called Israel and Judah, respectively, the prophets spent little time foretelling or predicting the future. Most of their energy was spent on forthtelling (see chapter 1 for an explanation of forthtelling). One prophet from this era, Gad, is referred to as David's "seer" (1 Chronicles 21:9). He served as God's mouthpiece, bringing the word of the Lord to David during the latter years of Saul's reign and in the early part of David's.

During this time, the prophets mostly scrutinized the actions of Israel's kings and criticized them when they veered from God's law or led the people into sin. For example, Samuel chastised Saul, Israel's first king—whom Samuel himself had anointed—for disobeying the Lord. The prophet Nathan condemned David for his adulterous relationship with Bathsheba (2 Samuel 12:1–14). Elijah was critical of Ahab (1 Kings 18:18). Some kings listened to these God-inspired prophets; many, sadly, did not.

over you wherever you go, and I will bring you back to this land. I will not leave you until I have done what I have promised you." (Genesis 28:13–15)

Later, when the twelve tribes found themselves enslaved in Egypt, God called Moses to lead them out. The promise if he would obey? "And I will bring you to the land I swore with uplifted hand to give to Abraham, to Isaac and to Jacob. I will give it to you as a possession. I am the LORD" (Exodus 6:8).

Theologians, scholars, and preachers are divided on whether these prophecies about the Promised Land have yet been fulfilled. Some say they were in ancient history, when Israel settled the Promised Land under Joshua (see Joshua 21:43–45). Others say these prophecies have only been *partially* fulfilled, as the Jewish people have never possessed the land all the way to the boundaries set forth by God in Genesis 15:18–21. This second group believes, however, that these promises *will* be completely fulfilled in the future (see Ezekiel 45–48 and Amos 9:14–15)—because God keeps every word of every promise He

Israeli banknote portrait of David Ben-Gurion, the first prime minister of the modern State of Israel. Many see its 1948 founding as an aspect of biblical prophecy.

makes. Many of them point to the decision by the United Nations in 1948 to partition Palestine and create an independent State of Israel as a key step toward the ultimate fulfillment of this land promise.

BEING CURSED

In His promise to Abraham and his descendants, God said, "Whoever curses you I will curse" (Genesis 12:3). If we broaden the idea of cursing to include mistreatment and physical harm, then Jewish history during both Bible times and modern times is filled with incidents in which the Jewish people have been "cursed" by others.

The Old Testament records Israel's domination by a long series of world empires: Egypt, Assyria, Babylonia, Medo-Persia, Greece,

The ancient Assyrians were a fierce people who overran the northern nation of Israel in 722 BC. Their ultimate demise and Israel's ultimate survival support belief in Bible prophecy.

Rome. The Bible also mentions mistreatment at the hands of numerous smaller tribes and nations.

One of history's most astounding and indisputable miracles is that the people of Israel have survived centuries of cursing and hostility. More than once the Jews have faced genocide. And yet they survive and even flourish to this day.

In 722 BC, the ten northern tribes were decimated by the Assyrian army. In 586 BC, the remaining two tribes in the south were plundered and taken into captivity by the Babylonians. When the Persians rose to power, a government official by the name of Haman tried to extinguish the Jewish people (see the book of Esther) and did not succeed.

After returning to their homeland, the Jewish remnant was subjugated by the Greeks and then savaged by the Romans in AD 70. Those who survived were scattered across the globe. Everywhere they went, the Jewish people were persecuted simply for being Jewish. In the 1930s and 1940s, the Nazi genocide claimed the lives of *six million* Jews. For their entire existence, the Jewish people have indeed been cursed by other peoples.

In chapter 3 we'll look more closely at the fulfillment of God's promise to curse Israel's enemies.

Soldiers like this one, depicted in Babylonian artwork, may have marched residents of Jerusalem into exile.

EXPERIENCING EXILE

Though God's promises to Abraham were unconditional, God made it clear on numerous occasions that if the Israelites wished to remain in the Promised Land, they would have to obey God's law. He would scatter them if they failed.

In Leviticus 26 we find God's long list of dire consequences for disobedience, including this prophecy: "I will scatter you among the nations" (verse 33). In Moses' farewell addresses to the nation found in the book of Deuteronomy, he warned of what would happen if the nation became corrupt in the land: "The LORD will scatter you among the peoples, and only a few of you will survive among the nations to which the LORD will drive you" (Deuteronomy 4:27). Just before his death, while reviewing the blessings that obedience would bring and the curses that would follow disobedience, Moses prophesied, "You

WOE, WOE, WOE!

The biblical prophets often announced oracles of woe—that is, announcements of divine anger. The Hebrew word for *woe* is *hoy*, which can be translated "Oh!" or "Alas!" or "Oy!" It's a reaction to something that prompts intense sorrow or distress. Typically, after a prophet proclaimed a woe, he or she spelled out the whys and whats for the coming discipline. An example of this form can be found in Amos 6:1, 7: "Woe to you who are complacent in Zion . . . you will be among the first to go into exile; your feasting and lounging will end" (Amos 6:1, 7).

will be uprooted from the land you are entering to possess. . . . Then the LORD will scatter you among all nations, from one end of the earth to the other" (Deuteronomy 28:63–64).

Other Old Testament prophets also predicted this coming exile. In Jeremiah's prophecy we read, "I will scatter them among nations that neither they nor their ancestors have known" (9:16). Ezekiel also spoke for God on this issue: "Also with uplifted hand I swore to them in the wilderness that I would disperse them among the nations and scatter them through the countries" (Ezekiel 20:23).

When were these dire prophecies of exile fulfilled?

In 722 BC, after refusing to heed the warnings of prophets such as Hosea and Amos, the northern kingdom of Israel was overrun by the Assyrians. As a result of this event and its aftermath, people often speak of the "lost tribes of Israel." In 586 BC, the Babylonians

Daniel, famed for his night in the lions' den, is known as an "exilic prophet" since he served during Judah's exile in Babylon.

43

invaded the southern kingdom of Judah, devastated Jerusalem, and took many of its residents into exile. This, too, was after the people of Judah dismissed the prophetic calls to repent.

These events effectively brought an end to the Jewish monarchy. However, they also paved the way for the ministries of more prophets—the prophets of the exile, such as Daniel and Ezekiel. Through these men, God offered His exiled people more hope and direction.

JUDGMENT COMES AT LAST

Here's how the Bible describes the fulfillment of all those prophecies of exile:

The LORD, the God of their ancestors, sent word to them through his messengers again and again, because he had pity on his people and on his dwelling place. But they mocked God's messengers, despised his words and scoffed at his prophets until the wrath of the LORD was aroused against his people and there was no remedy. He brought up against them the king of the Babylonians, who killed their young men with the sword in the sanctuary, and did not spare young men or young women, the elderly or the infirm. God gave them all into the hands of Nebuchadnezzar. He carried to Babylon all the articles from the temple of God, both large and small, and the treasures of the LORD's temple and the treasures of the king and his officials. They set fire to God's temple and broke down the wall of Jerusalem; they burned all the palaces and destroyed everything of value there. He carried into exile to Babylon the remnant, who escaped from the sword, and they became servants to him and his successors until the kingdom of Persia came to power. The land enjoyed its sabbath rests; all the time of its desolation it rested, until the seventy years were completed in fulfillment of the word of the LORD spoken by Jeremiah. (2 Chronicles 36:15–21)

They explained why destruction had come to them, and they pointed to a coming Messiah who would rescue Israel and restore the kingdom.

Ezekiel was (and still is) famous for speaking for God through vivid language and dramatic, theatrical acts. When talking to the people, he referenced a messianic figure who would "tend them and be their shepherd" (34:23), a "servant" (37:24) and "a shoot from the very top of a cedar," which the Lord would break off and plant "on the mountain heights of Israel" (17:22–23).

Daniel's messianic visions featured "one like a son of man, coming with the clouds of heaven" (Daniel 7:13). We'll discuss these messianic prophecies in a later chapter, but many interpreters are

Jesus echoed Daniel's prophecy when He said, "All the peoples of the earth will mourn when they see the Son of Man coming on the clouds of heaven, with power and great glory" (Matthew 24:30).

convinced Daniel's prophecy predicted the precise time of the Messiah's arrival, how He would deal with sin, how He would die, and how Jerusalem and its rebuilt temple would one day be destroyed.

The scattering of people from Judah and Israel had not yet taken place *throughout the entire world* (Deuteronomy 28:64), but with the Assyrian and Babylonian invasions, this process had begun.

RETURNING TO THEIR HOMELAND

The declarations of the prophets weren't restricted to doom, gloom, and woe. They also spoke of a time when God's people would be restored to their inheritance after a period of exile.

Isaiah relayed this divine promise: "Do not be afraid, for I am with you; I will bring your children from the east and gather you from the west" (43:5). Jeremiah put it like this: "I myself will gather the remnant of my flock out of all the countries where I have driven them and will bring them back to their pasture, where they will be fruitful and increase in number" (Jeremiah 23:3). Likewise, the prophet Ezekiel revealed this word from the Lord: "I will gather you from the nations and bring you back from the countries where you have been scattered, and I will give you back the land of Israel again" (Ezekiel 11:16–17).

Again, some maintain that these prophecies were fulfilled in 538 BC when King Cyrus gave permission for the Jews to return home. Others believe that event was only a partial fulfillment—that the prophecies will be fully realized in the future. Regardless of which

interpretation is correct, the prophets were clear on this fact: it would only be because of God's grace, faithfulness, and power that the Jewish people would be restored to their homeland.

One example of ancient prophecy over which there is no debate is Isaiah's specific prediction, 150 years before the fact, that a King Cyrus of Persia would authorize the Jews to return to their homeland and rebuild Jerusalem and the temple. "Cyrus . . . is my shepherd and will accomplish all that I please; he will say of Jerusalem, 'Let it be rebuilt,' and of the temple, 'Let its foundations be laid'" (Isaiah 44:28). This prediction came to pass in 538 BC exactly as the prophet said.

The prophet Isaiah spoke both harsh and gentle truths to God's people—but only after a seraph purified his lips with a hot coal (see Isaiah 6:5–7). The stained glass scene is from Brussels, Belgium.

Regarding Israel's exile and return, God allowed His people to be scattered when they broke their covenant with Him. He brought them home in order to fulfill that ancient prophecy involving Abraham: "You will be a blessing...and all peoples on earth will be blessed through you" (Genesis 12:1–3).

What about that divine promise that Abraham would be a blessing to all nations? To what degree or extent has this prophecy been fulfilled in history?

BLESSING ALL NATIONS

Throughout history, the Jewish people have made countless contributions to the world, including such things as the teddy bear, the modern ballpoint pen, color photography, and the polio vaccine. But the greatest blessings of Abraham and his descendants have been spiritual—giving the world (a) the truth of holy scripture and (b) a Savior.

Before the writings of the Old Testament had been completed and compiled—and before Christ had arrived—there was a golden era of ancient Israel. It occurred when the kingdom of Israel was united under kings Saul, David, and Solomon. In fact, it was during Solomon's reign that Israel enjoyed unparalleled prominence, influence, and peace. The writer of 1 Kings described one of the ways Israel was a blessing to the nations at that time: "King Solomon was greater in riches and wisdom than all the other kings of the earth. *The whole world sought audience with Solomon to hear the wisdom God had put in his heart*" (1 Kings 10:23–24, emphasis added). Indeed, the world continues to be blessed with the wisdom God gave Solomon—through the poetical books of the Old Testament: Proverbs, Ecclesiastes, and Song of Songs.

After their return from exile, the Jewish people completed the process of gathering the scriptures that God had inspired their leaders, priests, and prophets to write. The result was the blessing that we now call the Old Testament. This was the Bible Jesus used. His mostly Jewish followers, of course, wrote the New Testament documents later in the first century.

Many people would vehemently disagree that the Bible ever was or is a blessing to the world. They would point out that it has been misused to justify all sorts of terrible things, such as slavery and the mistreatment of women.

The nation of Israel produced the Messiah, Jesus, who would offer salvation to all—including the wise men who traveled from the east to offer Him gifts of gold, frankincense, and myrrh.

The Bible's teachings, however, have also been responsible for much good. As noted in *The World's Greatest Book*, "There's no way to know how many hospitals and schools have been built or how many charitable nonprofits and food banks have been established because of the Bible's injunctions to care for strangers, orphans, and widows (Deuteronomy 24:17, 19) and to 'love your neighbor' (Leviticus 19:18)."[1] And let's not forget that abolitionists were inspired by the Bible to oppose slavery in the mid-1800s. By almost any objective standard, the Bible has had a profoundly positive impact on the arts, educational systems, and politics of Western culture. The Hebrew scriptures are indeed a gift and blessing to the world.

The other primary way Abraham and his descendants have blessed the world is through the person of Christ. *This* is the good news that Christians believe: "Scripture foresaw that God would justify the Gentiles by faith, and announced the gospel in advance to Abraham: 'All nations will be blessed through you'" (Galatians 3:8). Christians—and remember, the very first Christians were Jewish—have always believed that Jesus of Nazareth was and is the Messiah prophesied in the Old Testament. The Christian view is that the entire Old Testament points to Jesus as the Savior sent by God to reconcile sinful humanity to Himself. Christians see Jesus as the ultimate blessing of the prophecy given to Abraham. We'll explore this topic of messianic prophecy in greater detail in chapter 6.

Many people start reading all the "woes" expressed by the Old Testament prophets—all those graphic descriptions of destruction—and think, *This prophecy stuff is too grim. Maybe I'll flip forward or backward a few books to a more encouraging section of scripture.*

Do this and you'll miss some startling descriptions of a period when justice and righteousness will flourish, and when peace and joy will abound on the earth. We get glimpses of this when Moses proclaimed, "The LORD reigns for ever and ever" (Exodus 15:18). What will this kingdom of God look like when it is finally and fully realized? The prophets provided a number of descriptions for this time.

Global peace: Isaiah said, "He will judge between the nations and will settle disputes for many peoples. They will beat their swords into plowshares and their spears into pruning hooks. Nation will not take up sword against nation, nor will they train for war anymore" (Isaiah 2:4). The prophet went on to say that this harmony will even extend to the animal kingdom: "The wolf will live with the lamb, the leopard will lie down with the goat, the calf and the lion and the yearling together; and a little child will lead them" (Isaiah 11:6).

In western Poland, a statue titled *Christ the King* looks ahead to the day when Jesus vanquishes evil and rules the earth in perfect righteousness.

Joy and prosperity: "'They will come and shout for joy on the heights of Zion; they will rejoice in the bounty of the LORD— the grain, the new wine and the olive oil, the young of the flocks and herds. They will be like a well-watered garden, and they will sorrow no more. Then young women will dance and be glad, young men and old as well. I will turn their mourning into gladness; I will give them comfort and joy instead of sorrow. I will satisfy the priests with abundance, and my people will be filled with my bounty,' declares the LORD" (Jeremiah 31:12–14).

Restoration and health: "Then will the eyes of the blind be opened and the ears of the deaf unstopped. Then will the lame leap like a deer, and the mute tongue shout for joy. Water will gush forth in the wilderness and streams in the desert" (Isaiah 35:5–6).

The renewal and fruitfulness of the earth: "'The days are coming,' declares the LORD, 'when the reaper will be overtaken by the plowman and the planter by the one treading grapes. New wine will drip from the mountains and flow from all the hills'" (Amos 9:13).

Twenty-two combines reap a grain field in Brazil. Biblical prophets talk of a day when God will make the earth so fruitful that seedtime and harvest overlap.

God's absolute, perfect rule: "The LORD will be king over the whole earth. On that day there will be one LORD, and his name the only name" (Zechariah 14:9).

The knowledge of God: "For the earth will be filled with the knowledge of the glory of the LORD as the waters cover the sea" (Habakkuk 2:14).

Are these beautiful descriptions pointing to a literal thousand-year reign of Christ on the earth after He comes again? Some Christians think so, citing Revelation 20:11–15, among other verses. Others believe these prophecies to be figurative descriptions of the spiritual rule of Christ in the hearts of His people. Whatever one concludes, the New Testament clearly claims that Christ is Lord and that He will return to vanquish evil and restore all things.

In the next chapter we'll look at some biblical prophecies against Israel's enemies that have been fulfilled.

HANG IN THERE!

Don't get discouraged if biblical prophecy at times seems like an impossible-to-understand puzzle.

Many people have spent decades studying these ancient and cryptic passages and still scratch their heads over the possible meanings. Ask God to give you ears to hear and eyes to see. Then study hard and read carefully and prayerfully. Even if many details remain a mystery, you can still find comfort and hope in the God who stands behind these prophecies, and you can still live with holy intention. Most experts will tell you that with the Holy Spirit's guidance and with diligent study, the puzzle *will* begin to make sense.

ENDNOTES

1   Lawrence H. Schiffman, Jerry Pattengale, eds., *The World's Greatest Book* (Franklin, TN: Worthy Books, 2017), 9.

Chapter 3:
PROPHECIES ABOUT OTHER NATIONS

One of the first sentences children learn to say is "That's not fair!" Kids make this declaration even though they don't take preschool classes in jurisprudence. Clearly, humans have an innate sense of right and wrong. As creatures made in the image of God, we can spot injustice a mile away. It infuriates us when a strong person takes advantage of the weak—and avoids any consequences for such misbehavior.

Thankfully, we don't have to spend our lives settling scores, seeking revenge, or living as vigilantes. God is just (Deuteronomy 32:4). He sees everything and everybody (Psalm 33:13). And, speaking of our unjust world, He has promised to rectify every wrong.

In chapter 2, we talked briefly about God's promises to Abraham. Do you remember that one of those guarantees was to curse all those who cursed Abraham or his descendants?

In this chapter we will look at some specific fulfillments of that promise—the notable nations or empires that have experienced divine retribution in history because of overt hostility toward God's people.

AMALEK

The Amalekites were a nomadic tribe in the Negev desert, which is to the south of Israel. Their patriarch was Amalek, the grandson of Esau who was the grandson of Abraham. The Amalekites were thus related to the Israelites. And yet they often allied themselves with other area tribes such as the Midianites, Moabites, Ammonites, and Edomites to oppose the descendants of Jacob—the Israelites. The first such occasion occurred at Rephidim, after the Israelites

This sculpture from a German church depicts a scene from Israel's history with Amalek: Moses' arms are held aloft by his brother, Aaron, and a man named Hur, while Joshua leads the army in battle. As long as Moses' arms were up, the Israelites prevailed (see Exodus 17:8–13).

had left Egypt and were moving toward the Promised Land (Exodus 17:8–15; see also Deuteronomy 25:17–19).

Later, when the Moabite king Balak summoned the prophet-diviner Balaam to curse Israel, he instead cursed Moab and prophesied, "Amalek was first among the nations, but their end will be utter destruction" (Numbers 24:20).

The Amalekites continued to be a thorn in the side of Israel when the nation was ruled by judges (Judges 6:3) and later when the Israelites were ruled by kings (1 Samuel 15:1–3; 30:1–20)

During King Hezekiah's reign, the remnant of Amalekites living in the hill country of Seir was killed by a group of warriors from the tribe of Simeon (1 Chronicles 4:41–43).

PHILISTIA

The Philistines were a militant coastal tribe in southwestern Palestine. Philistia was less like a nation and more like a coalition of the city-states Gaza, Ashkelon, Ashdod, Ekron, and Gath. These fortified cities were ruled by lords, not kings (see 1 Samuel 5:11). The Philistines are mentioned first in Genesis 10:14. They appear again in Exodus 15:14, where they are described as being wary and fearful of the Hebrew tribes that had been recently liberated from Egypt. That would explain their eventual hostility toward the Israelites.

Before Israel existed, Abraham spent much time in Philistia (Genesis 21:34), as did his son Isaac (Genesis 26). During the period of the judges, the Philistines were constantly hostile to the Israelites (see Judges 3; 10; 13–16). And they continued as long-term, bitter enemies during the reigns of

The Israelite "judge" (or deliverer) Samson concludes his ongoing battle with the Philistines by collapsing their crowded temple. More than three thousand people, including Samson himself, died (see Judges 16).

Saul and David. It's worth noting that the Philistines are mentioned 116 times in 1 and 2 Samuel.

Eventually, Jeremiah—who became a prophet around 626 BC when Josiah was king—predicted, "For the day has come to destroy all the Philistines and to remove all survivors who could help Tyre and Sidon. The Lᴏʀᴅ is about to destroy the Philistines, the remnant from the coasts of Caphtor" (Jeremiah 47:4). Zephaniah (Zephaniah 2:4–7) also prophesied the Philistines' doom.

Around 600 BC, God used King Nebuchadnezzar of Babylon to crush this aggressive people who worshiped the gods Dagon, Ashtoreth, and Baal-Zebub.

MOAB

Moab was a small kingdom on the southeastern edge of the Dead Sea, just north of the land of Edom. The people there were called Moabites. They were the descendants of Moab, who was the child born as a result of Lot's incestuous relationship with his oldest daughter (Genesis 19:30–37). You may recall that Ruth, the heroine of the Old Testament book of Ruth, was a Moabite (Ruth 1:4). She, by her marriage to Boaz, became the great-grandmother of Israel's King David.

God put Israel in a kind of national, forty-year "time out" because of the people's refusal to go into the Promised Land under Moses (Numbers 14:26–35). During this bleak period of wandering around the desert south of Canaan, the Israelites were forbidden to show hostility toward Moab (Deuteronomy 2:9). At the same time, God made it clear that the Moabites were forbidden from entering "the assembly of the LORD" (Deuteronomy 23:3; Nehemiah 13:1). Moreover, the Israelites were instructed, "Do not seek a treaty of friendship with them as long as you live" (Deuteronomy 23:6).

Despite Israel's neutral stance, Moab's King Balak declared war on the traveling Hebrews. He even summoned Balaam, a diviner, in hopes that he might put a curse on the Hebrews (Numbers 22:6; Joshua 24:9). Balak's plan backfired when Balaam cursed *Moab* instead.

The Moabites proved to be long-term enemies of Israel. They led the Israelites astray spiritually (see Numbers 25) and oppressed them during the period of the judges (Judges 3:12–30). Saul fought them (1 Samuel 14:47), and David did so, too, and even received tribute from them (1 Chronicles 18:2). At least one of King Solomon's foreign wives was from Moab (1 Kings 11:1). Perhaps this explains why such a "wise" king would build a place of worship for Chemosh, one of the gods worshiped in Moab (1 Kings 11:7, 33).

The Moabites were a proud (Isaiah 16:6) and idolatrous people, and multiple Old Testament writers prophesied their destruction: Isaiah 15–16; Jeremiah 48; Ezekiel 25:8–11; Amos 2:1–3.

In 585 BC, the mighty Babylonians brought an end to the Moabite nation.

EDOM

Abraham's long-awaited son, Isaac, married Rebekah. When she became pregnant, God told her, "Two nations are in your womb, and

...one people will be stronger than the other, and the older will serve the younger" (Genesis 25:23).

Rebekah gave birth to twin sons: Esau and Jacob. Sure enough, Jacob, the younger of the boys—through shrewdness and trickery—acquired his brother's birthright (Genesis 25:27–34) and blessing (Genesis 27).

Jacob became the father of the twelve tribes of Israel. Esau became the patriarch of the people of Edom, an area south of the Dead Sea known for its red soil. Edom means "red." Esau was sometimes called by this nickname because he sold his birthright to Jacob for a bowl of red soup (Genesis 25:30–34).

Twin brothers Jacob and Esau jostled each other in their mother's womb; later, the younger took advantage of the older's impulsiveness to obtain the family birthright. Jacob's descendants, the people of Israel, would face conflict with Esau's descendants, the Edomites, for centuries to come.

Because of their common roots, God had told Israel, "Do not despise an Edomite, for the Edomites are related to you" (Deuteronomy 23:7). If the Edomites ever received this same command from God, they ignored it; Esau passed his bitterness toward Jacob to his descendants. They chose to attack Israel on a regular basis.

As a result, King Saul warred against Edom (1 Samuel 14:47). King David eventually plundered them, "and all the Edomites became subject to David" (1 Chronicles 18:13). This fulfilled, at least in part, the prophecy God had given Rebekah.

Other prophets later foretold Edom's doom (Isaiah 21:11–12; Jeremiah 49:7–22; Ezekiel 25:12–14; 35:1–15; Joel 3:19; Amos 1:11–12; Obadiah 18; Malachi 1:2–5). Around 550 BC the Babylonians fulfilled these ancient predictions. Today, there is no trace of Edomite lineage or culture, whereas the Jewish nation is thriving.

AMMON

A nineteenth-century artist imagined sacrifices to the god Molek as looking like this. The Ammonites' hateful practices influenced the Israelites and brought strong condemnation from God's prophets.

The Ammonites descended from Lot's incestuous relationship with his younger daughter (see Genesis 19:38) and settled northeast of Moab. Their capital city was Rabbah—the site of modern-day Amman, the capital of Jordan. Following the Exodus and prior to the conquest of Canaan, God had told His people, "When you come to the Ammonites, do not harass them or provoke them to war, for I will not give you possession of any land belonging to the Ammonites. I have given it as a possession to the descendants of Lot" (Deuteronomy 2:19).

The people of Ammon were notorious for worshiping a fire god or sun god named Molek, also called Milcom. They did this by engaging in the unthinkable practice of child sacrifice (Leviticus 20:2–5; 1 Kings 11:7; 2 Kings 23:10). Infants would be sacrificed "in the fire" (2 Kings 17:17) while worshipers beat drums and shouted and danced around idols. The Ammonites named their god Molek probably because it stems from the Hebrew root word for "king"; the Ammonites saw Molek as their protector.

Despite being forbidden by God to engage in such practices (Leviticus 18:21), the Israelites indulged in this kind of pagan worship (see Judges 10:6). Such flagrant disobedience led to them being oppressed by the Ammonites (Judges 10–11), thus requiring deliverance by God at the hands of Jephthah. During the era when Israel was united, both Saul and David had conflict with the Ammonites (see 1 Samuel 11–12; 14:47; 2 Samuel 10; 12:26–31), although Solomon later took an Ammonite wife, Naamah, who became the mother of King Rehoboam (1 Kings 14:21). In the late seventh century BC, the Ammonites took perverse pleasure in taunting the suffering people of Judah (Zephaniah 2:8).

As happened with the Moabites, the prophets lined up to condemn the Ammonites and foretell their destruction (see Jeremiah 9:25–26; 25:21; 49:1–6; Ezekiel 21:28–32; 25:1–7; Amos 1:13–15). Sure enough, Rabbah was sacked by Nebuchadnezzar soon after the Babylonian invasion of Judah in 586 BC. Later, Arab invaders also took advantage of Rabbah. Following the campaign of Alexander the Great, Ammon was controlled by the Egyptian Ptolemies, the Seleucids, and then the Nabateans. Eventually Ammonite culture disappeared completely, leaving behind only a few archaeological ruins.

Mosaic of Alexander the Great, who overran Damascus in 332 BC.

DAMASCUS (SYRIA OR ARAM)

Damascus is first mentioned in the Bible in Genesis 14:15. According to the Jewish historian Josephus, it was founded by Uz, the son of Aram and great-grandson of Moses. Some 160 miles northeast of Jerusalem, Damascus figures prominently in the New Testament as the place where the newly converted Saul—also named Paul—met Ananias (see Acts 9). For thousands of years Damascus has been a major city of what is now Syria, which in ancient times was called Aram. Damascus is often described as the oldest city in the world. It is surely one of the most *resilient* cities in the world.

When announcing coming judgment on Israel's neighbors, the prophet Amos singled out Damascus for divine retribution. "This is what the LORD says: 'For three sins of Damascus, even for four, I will not relent. Because she threshed Gilead with sledges having iron teeth, I will send fire on the house of Hazael that will consume the fortresses of Ben-Hadad. I will break down the gate of Damascus'" (Amos 1:3–5).

Jewish historian Josephus was born a few years after the death and resurrection of Jesus, and he lived to around AD 100. His book *Antiquities of the Jews* provides insight into many aspects of the Bible

Isaiah predicted a similar outcome: "See, Damascus will no longer be a city but will become a heap of ruins" (Isaiah 17:1). Jeremiah added this judgment: "I will set fire to the walls of Damascus; it will consume the fortresses of Ben-Hadad" (Jeremiah 49:27).

Here is what we know from history: In 733 BC, the Assyrian army, under King Tiglath-Pileser III, invaded Syria. They captured Damascus and deported its people (2 Kings 16:9). In 605 BC, Babylon conquered Damascus. In 332 BC, Alexander the Great, the Grecian ruler, conquered Damascus.

Despite its violent history and multiple invasions, Damascus still stands. Does this mean the prophets were using hyperbole to get their points across? Or does this mean we need to look to the future to see an ultimate fulfillment? Scholars disagree on the answers to these questions.

TYRE

According to the historian Herodotus, Tyre, a Canaanite city in Phoenicia, north of Israel, was founded around 2700 BC. Located on the Mediterranean shoreline, the city included a small, well-fortified island just off the coast. Tyre is mentioned sixty times in the Bible and was even listed as part of the tribe of Asher's inheritance (see Joshua 19:29)—even though the Israelites never took possession of it (see 2 Samuel 24:7).

Tyre was a friendly trading partner when Israel was united (2 Samuel 5:11; 1 Kings 5:1–11). But in the later kingdom period, this alliance dissolved, and suddenly the prophets were issuing withering denunciations of this coastal commercial center:

✳ **Isaiah:** "A prophecy against Tyre: Wail, you ships of Tarshish! For Tyre is destroyed and left without house or harbor. From the land of Cyprus word has come to them" (Isaiah 23:1).

Modern-day Tyre may not be located on the site of the biblical city of the same name.

✳ **Jeremiah:** "Then send word to the kings of Edom, Moab, Ammon, Tyre and Sidon. . . . I will give all your countries into the hands of my servant Nebuchadnezzar king of Babylon; I will make even the wild animals subject to him" (Jeremiah 27:3, 6).

✳ **Ezekiel:** "I am against you, Tyre, and I will bring many nations against you, like the sea casting up its waves. They will destroy the walls of Tyre and pull down her towers; I will scrape away her rubble and make her a bare rock. Out in the sea she will become a place to spread fishnets, for I have spoken, declares the Sovereign LORD. She will become plunder for the nations" (Ezekiel 26:3–5). So great was Tyre's pride that Ezekiel went on to compare this city-state's arrogance (and fall) to Satan's (see chapter 28).

Shortly after Ezekiel's prophecy, according to the Jewish historian Josephus, Tyre was indeed besieged by Nebuchadnezzar between 587 and 574 BC. Nebuchadnezzar attacked only the mainland city, not the island off the coast. Some argue that Nebuchadnezzar's invasion was not, therefore, a fulfillment of the prophecy. Others note, however, that Ezekiel began his prophecy talking about "many nations." He then emphasized this idea with the phrase "they will destroy." In other words, though Nebuchadnezzar did not completely destroy Tyre, he was the first of many nations to come against it. Sure enough, in 332 BC, Alexander the Great used the ruins of mainland Tyre to build a causeway to the island portion of the city-state, which he then destroyed.

And yet, by the time of Jesus, the city and surrounding region had been rebuilt and had regained much of its former glory. In fact, the Gospel writers tell of Jesus exorcising and restoring a demon-possessed girl from this region (see Matthew 15:21–28; Mark 7:24–31).

Because of all this rebuilding, some accuse the prophet Ezekiel of inaccuracy, specifically because of his words "I will make you a bare rock, and you will become a place to spread fishnets. *You will never be rebuilt*, for I the LORD have spoken, declares the Sovereign LORD" (Ezekiel 26:14, emphasis added).

There *is* a modern-day Tyre, Lebanon; however, it is unlikely that what we see today is what Ezekiel meant by Tyre. Some conservative scholars argue that what was once mainland Tyre is now underwater. If that is the case, people *are* able to spread their fishing nets over her.

EGYPT

The words "Egypt," "Egyptian," and "Egyptians" are found almost 750 times in the Bible. That's because this nation just southwest of Israel is a major player in the story of God's people.

Genesis records how the family of Abraham ended up being "guests" in Egypt due to an extended drought/famine in Canaan. Exodus, the second book of the Bible, tells how the Hebrew people eventually became slaves there and how God used Moses to lead them to freedom.

Because of Egypt's mistreatment of the Hebrews and Pharaoh's hard-hearted refusal to let them go, Moses, acting prophetically, foretold a series of plagues that would come on the nation. These ten

Modern Cairo, capital of Egypt, is a city of some twenty million people in a nation of around ninety-seven million—less than the combined populations of California, Texas, Florida, and New York.

supernatural disasters were predicted and fulfilled in Exodus 7–12. As a result of these judgments, Pharaoh reluctantly let the Hebrew people go.

However, he then famously changed his mind and chased after them, pursuing them into and through the split-apart Red Sea. As per Moses' on-the-spot prophecy, the sea closed in on Pharaoh's army, drowning the Egyptians and ensuring Israel's freedom (Exodus 14:13–28).

At the time of Isaiah, there were some who wanted to look west to Egypt for protection from the great empire Assyria to the east. Isaiah, in chapters 19–20, speaking for God, scoffed at the idea, saying, "The wise counselors of Pharaoh give senseless advice" (19:11). He gave a grim vision of Egypt's future. "'I will hand the Egyptians over to the power of a cruel master, and a fierce king will rule over them,' declares the Lord, the Lᴏʀᴅ Almighty" (Isaiah 19:4).

To dramatically illustrate Egypt's coming humiliation, God had His prophet walk about barefoot and naked for three years. This was a picture of how "the king of Assyria will lead away stripped and barefoot the Egyptian captives

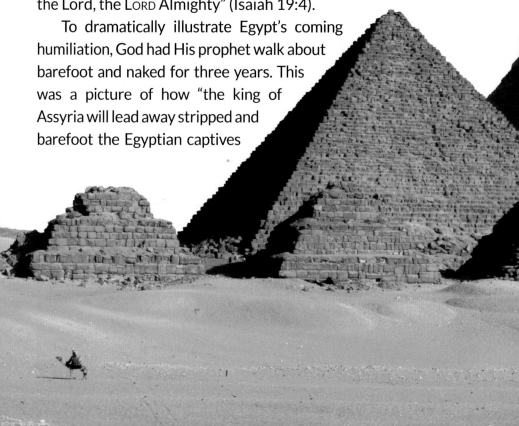

and Cushite exiles, young and old, with buttocks bared—to Egypt's shame" (Isaiah 20:4).

Later in Judah's history, as the Babylonians were closing in on Jerusalem, the people again were looking to Egypt for rescue. In Ezekiel 29–32, the prophet pointed out the futility of trusting in such an impotent "savior," saying to the Egyptians, "You have been a staff of reed for the people of Israel. When they grasped you with their hands, you splintered and you tore open their shoulders; when they leaned on you, you broke and their backs were wrenched. Therefore this is what the Sovereign Lord says: I will bring a sword against you and kill both man and beast. Egypt will become a desolate wasteland" (29:6–9).

Sure enough, Nebuchadnezzar conquered the "weak reed" of Egypt around 605 BC (see Jeremiah 43:8–13; 46:1–25; Ezekiel 29:17–21). As for Egypt's future, God declared through Ezekiel, "At the end of forty years I will gather the Egyptians from the nations where they were scattered. I will bring them back from captivity and return them to Upper Egypt, the land of their ancestry. There they will be a lowly kingdom. It will be the lowliest of kingdoms and will never again exalt itself

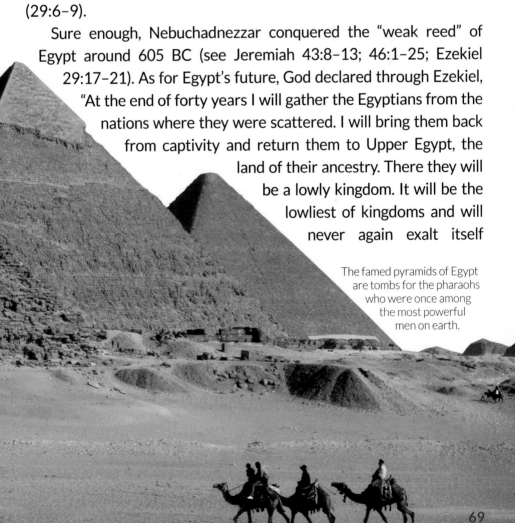

The famed pyramids of Egypt are tombs for the pharaohs who were once among the most powerful men on earth.

above the other nations. I will make it so weak that it will never again rule over the nations" (Ezekiel 29:13–15).

Historians agree that Egypt has never come close to attaining the prestige and power it once enjoyed.

CUSH/ETHIOPIA

The Upper Nile region south of Egypt (northern Sudan) was known variously as Cush, Nubia, or Ethiopia. In Isaiah 18:1–7, we read a prophetic announcement against these fearsome, "aggressive" (verse 2) people who lived in "the land of whirring wings" (verse 1). Isaiah's prophecy most likely indicated that because of its alliances with Egypt, Cush would face judgment along with Egypt.

ASSYRIA

A fearsome world power in the ancient Near East until the seventh century BC, Assyria figures prominently in biblical history (mostly in 2 Kings 15–23). This ancient empire was situated in what is today northern Iraq. It was the pagan kingdom used by God to bring judgment on the northern kingdom of Israel, as foretold by prophets such as Isaiah: "Woe to the Assyrian, the rod of my anger, in whose hand is the club of my wrath!" (Isaiah 10:5).

After steamrolling the northern kingdom's ten tribes and scattering the people (see 2 Kings 15:19–20, 29; 17:3–41), the Assyrians under Sennacherib wanted more. They set their sights on the southern kingdom of Judah as well. For a time, King Hezekiah was able to "buy off" his enemies with large payments of silver and gold (2 Kings 18:13–16). However, when the Assyrian leaders began to taunt the people and mock God (2 Kings 18:17–37), Hezekiah prayed boldly and desperately: "Now, Lord our God, deliver us from his hand,

WHAT ABOUT UNFULFILLED PROPHECIES?

Skeptics have always tried to discredit the truth of the Bible by claiming certain prophecies were never fulfilled as predicted and, therefore, the Bible is not to be trusted. It is true that many prophecies in scripture, even ancient ones in the Old Testament, have not yet been fulfilled; however, there's a reason for this.

In some cases, the fulfillment of a certain prophecy was (or is) dependent on a human response. The people of God were told on multiple occasions to repent. If they did, certain prophecies of destruction would not come to pass. Similarly, if God's people disobeyed, they would miss out on divine blessings. Leviticus 26:3–12, for example, went unfulfilled because God's people did not keep the covenant promises they made to God.

Certain biblical prophecies, such as the second coming of Christ, refer to events obviously in the future. Others, on careful inspection, are fulfilled in stages—something known as "developmental fulfillment." For example, Genesis 3:15 announced that God, in restoring creation after humanity's sin, would cause the serpent's head to be crushed. Near the end of His life, Jesus suggested that His crucifixion would be a partial fulfillment of this prophecy (John 12:31–32), but it will ultimately be fulfilled when the serpent Satan is thrown into the bottomless pit, or Abyss, as described in Revelation 20:3.

Closely related to developmental fulfillment is "prophetic telescoping." Consider what happens when you view a massive mountain range from a distance. The peak of one mountaintop may seem to be just in front of or just behind another, when in reality a great distance separates them.

Prophecy often operates in a similar way. In many cases, long periods can separate prophetic events. To the prophet, certain prophetic events may have looked as though they were going to take place in immediate succession, when in fact God intended a gap of time between them.

In other cases, prophecies have been fulfilled, but scholars have as yet been unable to connect historical events to them. We may not have historical or archaeological evidence yet to verify a prophecy's fulfillment, or we may not know about events that happened in history.

"Forty more days and Nineveh will be overthrown," Jonah shouted in the Assyrian capital (Jonah 3:4). When the people heard the message and repented, the prophecy went unfulfilled.

so that all the kingdoms of the earth may know that you alone, LORD, are God" (2 Kings 19:19).

God heard Hezekiah's petition. He sent Isaiah to prophesy the good news that He would deliver Jerusalem and punish Assyria (2 Kings 19:32–34). And Hezekiah and the people of God didn't have to wait long. That very night God did as He promised, striking down 185,000 Assyrian troops! The king of Assyria returned to Nineveh, the capital city of Assyria. Later, when he was worshiping his god Nisrok, he was murdered by his own sons (2 Kings 19:37).

The prophets Isaiah and Nahum saw Assyria's certain demise and announced it *well in advance*:

Assyria's King Sennacherib is murdered by his own sons after returning home from Jerusalem, defeated by the angel of the Lord (see 2 Kings 19:20–37).

* Isaiah lived in the eighth century BC, but he wrote, "[The Lord] will punish the king of Assyria for the willful pride of his heart and the haughty look in his eyes" (Isaiah 10:12).

* "The Lord Almighty has sworn, 'Surely, as I have planned, so it will be, and as I have purposed, so it will happen. I will crush the Assyrian in my land; on my mountains I will trample him down. His yoke will be taken from my people, and his burden removed from their shoulders'" (Isaiah 14:24–25).

* "The Lord is good, a refuge in times of trouble. He cares for those who trust in him, but with an overwhelming flood he will make an end of Nineveh; he will pursue his foes into the realm of darkness" (Nahum 1:7–8).

By 612 BC, the mighty Babylonians had become the new power in the ancient Near East. They defeated the brutal Assyrians and destroyed Nineveh. The Babylonians so thoroughly decimated Nineveh that its ruins weren't found by archaeologists until 1845. It was never rebuilt. In time the Babylonians would become the second great empire to be used by God to deal with His wayward people.

In the midst of all those dire Old Testament prophecies, we find some striking words in Isaiah: "In that day there will be a highway from Egypt to Assyria. The Assyrians will go to Egypt and the Egyptians to Assyria. The Egyptians and Assyrians will worship together. In that day Israel will be the third, along with Egypt and Assyria, a blessing on the earth. The Lord Almighty will bless them, saying, 'Blessed be Egypt my people, Assyria my handiwork, and Israel my inheritance'" (Isaiah 19:23–25).

We must remember that what Isaiah called Assyria includes modern-day Syria, Iraq, and Iran. Some scholars argue that this prophecy must point to some literal fulfillment in the future, when all nations will worship the Messiah in His peaceful kingdom. Others say it was fulfilled following the ministry of Jesus, when the Gospel was preached and individuals from various nations put their faith in Jesus as the Christ (see Acts 2:9–11). Which is it? Will Isaiah's "highway" be a literal road? Again, there's no consensus. Some say yes. Others treat this "highway" as a metaphor signifying a time of supernatural cooperation and peace.

BABYLON

The empire dominating the world stage for much of the seventh and sixth centuries BC (following the demise of Assyria) was Babylonia. Its capital city was

Babylon, some fifty miles south of modern-day Baghdad, Iraq. It was situated on the Euphrates River, two hundred miles above that waterway's intersection with the Tigris. Genesis 10:8–10 names Nimrod as the founder of Babylon.

Babylon reached the peak of its power and influence under King Nebuchadnezzar. Then God used it as His instrument in the early sixth century BC to punish the inhabitants of Judah for their covenantal unfaithfulness. Here is a brief description of those dark days:

> The LORD, the God of their ancestors, sent word to them through his messengers again and again, because he had pity on his people and on his dwelling place. But they mocked God's

Babylon was the undisputed world power of its day—until the Medes and Persians took over, as prophesied by Isaiah. This 1819 painting is titled *The Fall of Babylon: Cyrus the Great Defeating the Chaldean Army.*

messengers, despised his words and scoffed at his prophets until the wrath of the LORD was aroused against his people and there was no remedy. He brought up against them the king of the Babylonians, who killed their young men with the sword in the sanctuary, and did not spare young men or young women, the elderly or the infirm. God gave them all into the hands of Nebuchadnezzar. He carried to Babylon all the articles from the temple of God, both large and small, and the treasures of the LORD's temple and the treasures of the king and his officials. They set fire to God's temple and broke down the wall of Jerusalem; they burned all the palaces and destroyed everything of value there. He carried into exile to Babylon the remnant, who escaped from the sword, and they became servants to him and his successors until the kingdom of Persia came to power. The land enjoyed its sabbath rests; all the time of its desolation it rested, until the seventy years were completed in fulfillment of the word of the LORD spoken by Jeremiah. (2 Chronicles 36:15–21)

Habakkuk was one of the prophets who saw and lamented the great evil among his people. And yet he had a hard time understanding how or why God would use a godless empire like Babylonia to address the sins of the Israelites. He asked God, "Why are you

The prophet Habakkuk appears sad and confused in this fifteenth-century statue from famed sculptor Donatello.

silent while the wicked swallow up those more righteous than themselves?" (1:13).

Habakkuk was told to wait for God to resolve such matters. In short, God would punish Babylon in His own time.

Isaiah foretold the destruction of Babylon: "See, I will stir up against them the Medes, who do not care for silver and have no delight in gold" (Isaiah 13:17). He encouraged the people to take up this taunt against the king of Babylon: "How the oppressor has come to an end! How his fury has ended! The LORD has broken the rod of the wicked, the scepter of the rulers" (Isaiah 14:4–5).

Historians tell us that in 539 BC Babylon fell to the Persians. The following year, King Cyrus gave permission for the Jewish people to return to Israel.

Scholars debate whether Isaiah's prophecy was completely fulfilled, is yet to be fulfilled, or is one of those prophecies that will involve a dual fulfillment. It's true that the Babylon of Isaiah's time did fall to the Persians. However, Isaiah prophesied categorically that Babylon "will never be inhabited or lived in through all generations" (13:20). Since Babylon has never been completely uninhabited, this would seem to point to a future fulfillment.

Then there is the added fact that Babylon reappears in Revelation (see Revelation 14:8; 16:19; 17–18). For those who accept a futurist interpretation of Revelation—that Revelation's prophecies point to events at the end of the world—there are two common understandings of this new, future Babylon: (1) It is a symbol for a selfish world in total rebellion against God. (2) It represents the literal political, economic, and religious empire of the coming Antichrist. According to this view, God was revealing to John, Revelation's author, that this future version of Babylon will be destroyed when Christ returns (Revelation 18:2).

PERSIA

In 586 BC, the Babylonians invaded Judah and decimated Jerusalem. They destroyed Solomon's temple and took the people of Judah captive.

The Cyrus Cylinder, on display at the British Museum, details the Persian king's conquest of Babylon and may hint at Cyrus's decision to allow the Jews to rebuild their ruined temple in Jerusalem.

More than a century before Cyrus became king of Persia, the prophet Isaiah called him by name and predicted that he would rebuild Jerusalem. In 538 BC, exactly as Isaiah foretold, Cyrus announced that God had told him to rebuild the temple (Ezra 1:2; 6:3). Cyrus was not even a worshiper of Israel's God. Thus, his decree demonstrates that God can and does use unlikely people for His purposes (Isaiah 45:1–4).

What happened to Persia in history? In Daniel 8:1–8, 20–22, Daniel was given a vision in which a powerful, two-horned ram charged west and north and south doing as it pleased. Suddenly a shaggy goat appeared from the west, charged the ram, and "knocked it to the ground and trampled on it." The angel Gabriel then revealed to Daniel that the two-horned ram represented the kings of Media and Persia, and the goat represented the king of Greece. This prophecy was fulfilled in 333 BC when Alexander the Great conquered the Persians and Greece became the world's next great empire.

ARABIA

Biblical Arabia was the large peninsula to the southeast of Israel. It was surrounded on three sides by water (the Red Sea on the southwest, the Indian Ocean on the south, and the Persian Gulf on the east). To the north of Arabia was the Fertile Crescent, today's Jordan and Iraq.

In 2 Chronicles 9:14, the kings of Arabia are mentioned as bringing gold and silver to King Solomon. But in Isaiah 21:13–17, the prophet was declaring an oracle of divine judgment on the people of Arabia. In Jeremiah the kings of Arabia are mentioned in a long list of Israel's enemies (25:24).

In about 715 BC, the Assyrians overran this area as part of their campaign to conquer Egypt.

As leader of Nazi Germany, Adolf Hitler caused almost unimaginable suffering in the early twentieth century. But his "thousand-year reich," built largely on hatred of Jewish people, lasted about twenty-two years.

SUMMARY

Looking at this long list of nations punished by God in history, it's difficult to draw any other conclusion than this one: God is just. He will not tolerate disobedience forever. All people will one day be judged.

Why does this matter to modern-day followers of Jesus? What can we take away from reading about these fulfilled prophecies? At least three truths:

* We don't have to take vengeance on others. That's God's job.
* We don't have to fret about bullies getting away with their misdeeds. God sees evil and He will right every injustice.
* We don't have to wonder if God will keep His word. He keeps every promise He makes.

Chapter 4:

PROPHECIES ABOUT GOD'S COVENANT PROMISES

Many Bible prophecies are overt promises from God. In this chapter we'll take a brief look at the eternally significant agreements God made with Adam, Noah, Abraham, and David—and we'll wrestle with what those covenants mean to us.

As we begin, let's ask and answer a few questions.

WHAT DO WE MEAN BY THE TERM COVENANT?

The Hebrew word from which we get our English word *covenant* is *berit*. A covenant is a binding agreement or contract between

COVENANT THEOLOGY

For almost two thousand years, Christians have pored over the Old and New Testaments trying to understand God's dealings with humanity. One of the "systems" for explaining the plan and purposes of God is known as "covenant theology."

Covenant theology says that throughout human history God has established at least two different covenants: a covenant of works and a covenant of grace. Theologians who subscribe to this way of understanding the Bible see an uninterrupted progression from the Old to the New Testament. They don't view the Old Testament people of God, Israel, and the New Testament people of God, the church, as two distinct entities. Rather, covenant theologians see Israel and the church as one people all belonging to God. Based on this understanding, they believe the promises made to Israel in the Old Testament are also meant for the church today. According to this viewpoint, all believers are the "true Israel."

The French Reformer John Calvin (1509–1564) is considered a primary proponent of covenant theology.

two parties. In ancient times, covenants were often ratified or sealed by eating a meal together, swearing an oath, giving gifts, or establishing some sort of pillar or memorial—usually in the presence of eyewitnesses. (See Genesis 9:15; 21:30–31.) Entering into a covenant bound each party to carry out deeds on one another's behalf. We could think of a covenant as a solemn promise.

A careful reading of the Bible shows that God's dealings with humanity throughout history have involved a series of covenants. Redemption by God, relationship with God, a rich life from God—all these things come through covenants.

HOW MANY COVENANTS DOES THE BIBLE DESCRIBE?

As we might expect, there is no consensus among scholars on this question. Some say that we can explain all of God's actions in human history by one large covenant—a covenant of grace or redemption. These theologians recognize that the details vary at different times in history, but they believe that God has always been graciously calling a people to Himself.

However, others say that the overarching covenant of grace described above is being worked out through a series of subordinate covenants. They list as many as eight covenants: Adamic, Edenic, Noahic, Abrahamic, Mosaic, Palestinian, Davidic, and new. Careful readers note that some of these covenants are conditional or bilateral in nature, whereas others are unconditional or unilateral in nature.

The Mosaic covenant included the Ten Commandments God gave to Moses on Mount Sinai.

WHAT'S THE DIFFERENCE BETWEEN CONDITIONAL AND UNCONDITIONAL COVENANTS?

A conditional or bilateral covenant occurs when God promises to give significant blessings to individuals or to nations *if* they fulfill certain conditions or meet certain requirements.

An unconditional or unilateral covenant is a declaration of divine purpose with no strings attached. Unconditional covenants often begin with the words "I will." God declares His resolve to do what He has promised, regardless of any human's response.

Of the eight covenants in the Bible, six are unconditional: the Adamic, the Noahic, the Abrahamic, the Palestinian, the Davidic, and the new. The other two—the Edenic and the Mosaic—are conditional covenants.

HOW, IF AT ALL, DO THE BIBLICAL COVENANTS FIT TOGETHER?

Each covenant intensified and built on the previous covenant. Together they form the foundation of biblical prophecy. To understand with certainty that the Old and New Testament prophecies will come to pass, it is important to understand the seriousness of a covenant.

Let's look briefly now at the unique aspects of each covenant.

EDENIC COVENANT

This was the first covenant God made with humanity. It's found in the opening chapters of Scripture:

> Then God said, "Let us make mankind in our image, in our likeness, so that they may rule over the fish in the sea and the birds in the sky, over the livestock and all the wild animals, and over all the creatures that move along the ground."
>
> So God created mankind in his own image, in the image of God he created them; male and female he created them. God blessed them and said to them, "Be fruitful and increase in number; fill the earth and subdue it. Rule over the fish in the sea and the birds in the sky and over every living creature that moves on the ground."

Then God said, "I give you every seed-bearing plant on the face of the whole earth and every tree that has fruit with seed in it. They will be yours for food. And to all the beasts of the earth and all the birds in the sky and all the creatures that move along the ground—everything that has the breath of life in it—I give every green plant for food." And it was so. (Genesis 1:26–30)

Then we read: "And the LORD God commanded the man, 'You are free to eat from any tree in the garden; but you must not eat from the tree of the knowledge of good and evil, for when you eat from it you will certainly die'" (Genesis 2:16–17).

As we can see, under the Edenic covenant, God generously gave Adam, the patriarch of the human race, almost all of creation. God gave him the great privilege and responsibility to rule over the

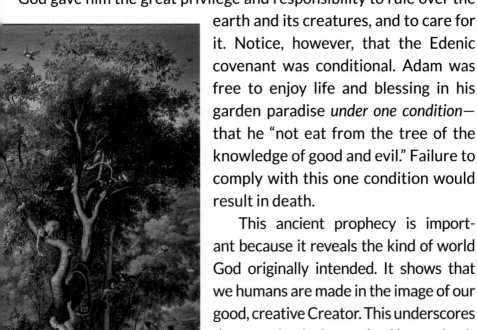

earth and its creatures, and to care for it. Notice, however, that the Edenic covenant was conditional. Adam was free to enjoy life and blessing in his garden paradise *under one condition*— that he "not eat from the tree of the knowledge of good and evil." Failure to comply with this one condition would result in death.

This ancient prophecy is important because it reveals the kind of world God originally intended. It shows that we humans are made in the image of our good, creative Creator. This underscores the great intrinsic worth of humanity. It

With the serpent looking on, Eve breaks the Edenic covenant by eating the forbidden fruit and offering a taste to Adam. This Johann Wenzel Peter painting is from the early 1800s.

also reveals God's generous desire to share His creation with us and for us to care for the world He has made. The Edenic covenant shows God giving great freedom but also giving a protective prohibition—a guardrail.

When Adam and his wife, Eve, broke this covenant (see Genesis 3:1–7), they were immediately filled with guilt, fear, and shame. And so, God put the Adamic covenant into place.

ADAMIC COVENANT

This was an unconditional covenant, a prophecy or divine announcement to humankind about what life would look like on earth going forward. There was no directive involved, no quid pro quo. It was simply a declaration by God.

To the serpent God said, "And I will put enmity between you and the woman, and between your offspring and hers; he will crush your head, and you will strike his heel."

To the woman God said, "I will make your pains in childbearing very severe; with painful labor you will give birth to children. Your desire will be for your husband, and he will rule over you."

To Adam God said, "Because you listened to your wife and ate fruit from the tree about which I commanded you, 'You must not eat from it,' cursed is the ground because of you; through painful toil you will eat food from it all the days of your life. It will produce thorns and thistles for you, and you will eat the plants of the field. By the sweat of your brow you will eat your

With the perspective of time, we understand something that would have been mysterious to Adam and Eve: Jesus would be the offspring of the woman who would crush the head of the serpent, Satan.

food until you return to the ground, since from it you were taken; for dust you are and to dust you will return" (Genesis 3:15–19).

Here, because of sin, God pronounced dire consequences and curses over His creation. Because of sin, the woman's lot would be to experience much pain and sorrow in motherhood and marriage. The man was told that he would have to toil and sweat until he would "return to the ground." In short, humanity's future would involve divorce courts, soul-killing jobs, funerals, and cemeteries.

But did you notice the glimmer of hope? There is the gracious hint of a coming redeemer in verse 15 about the woman's offspring crushing the head of the serpent. The Genesis narrative goes on to reveal how God took the lives of some animals so that Adam and Eve might cover up their nakedness with "garments of skin" (3:21). With the promise of a savior and the picture of a sacrifice, the man and woman were expelled from paradise and prevented from reentering (Genesis 3:21–24).

Adam and Eve's disobedience got them kicked out of the beautiful Garden of Eden and brought a host of hardships on them and every person to follow.

The Adamic covenant is important as we struggle with the results of sin all around us—and in us. We are reminded many times daily that we are fallen people living in a broken world. Relationships are hard. Parenting is hard. Work is hard. Intimacy with God is hard. And the mutiny in Eden is the reason why. The Adamic covenant reminds us that our sin does not escape God's notice. On the bright side, we are encouraged that God has always had a plan to rescue and restore His rebellious creatures.

WHAT IS DISPENSATIONAL THEOLOGY, OR DISPENSATIONALISM?

In theological circles, *dispensation* is used by some to refer to what they see as well-defined periods or distinguishable economies in God's unfolding plan for the world. In these distinctly different stages, humans are stewards under God and are tasked with new privileges and responsibilities. Dispensationalists see as many as seven such stages: innocence or freedom, conscience, human government, promise, law, grace, and kingdom. They do not use the words *dispensation* and *covenant* synonymously; they do not equate what they see as dispensations with the biblical covenants. On the contrary, they see the covenants God made with people such as Noah, Abraham, Moses, and David as fitting into these various dispensational periods. Think of it this way: a dispensation has to do with distinct periods, whereas a covenant involves definitive promises.

Dispensational theology is distinctive from covenant theology in two primary ways: (1) dispensationalists tend to interpret scripture more literally; and (2) they see Israel and the church as two distinct peoples, for whom God has distinct purposes. So, for example, when the prophets foretell a glorious earthly kingdom for Israel (Isaiah 60–62), dispensationalists take this at face value. They do not see such prophecies as being fulfilled by the church in a "spiritual" way.

Cyrus Ingerson Scofield (1843–1921) edited a study Bible that popularized dispensational theology in the early twentieth century.

After the flood, Noah and his family sacrifice to God under the rainbow, the symbol of God's covenant never again to destroy the earth with a flood.

NOAHIC COVENANT

In the unfolding story of God and His world, we see the acceleration of sin and evil. Adam and Eve's first child, Cain, becomes a murderer, taking the life of his younger brother. According to Genesis 6:5, "The LORD saw how great the wickedness of the human race had become on the earth, and that every inclination of the thoughts of the human heart was only evil all the time."

"But," Genesis tells us, "Noah found favor in the eyes of the LORD" (6:8). The Hebrew word translated as "favor" in that verse literally means "grace." Noah was graced by God.

Noah's story is familiar, even to people who seldom read the Bible. God decided to judge the world and start over. He commanded Noah to build a big boat called an ark. He did so, filling it with his family and with animals, "two of every kind" (Genesis 6:20). Then God sent a great flood to, in effect, wash the earth clean.

After Noah, his family, and the animals departed the ark, the Lord made a covenant with Noah—actually, with all humankind.

In Genesis 9 we read the details of the Noahic covenant:

* God blesses Noah and repeats the command He had previously given to Adam: "Be fruitful and increase in number and fill the earth" (verse 1).

* He expands humanity's diet, saying: "Everything that lives and moves about will be food for you. Just as I gave you the green plants, I now give you everything" (verse 3).

* Some see a provision for human government in the statement "Whoever sheds human blood, by humans shall their blood be shed; for in the image of God has God made mankind" (verse 6).

* God makes a promise to the human race and offers a sign of His commitment to keep His promise:

> "I establish my covenant with you: Never again will all life be destroyed by the waters of a flood; never again will there be a flood to destroy the earth."
>
> And God said, "This is the sign of the covenant I am making between me and you and every living creature with you, a covenant for all generations to come: I have set my rainbow in the clouds, and it will be the sign of the covenant between me and the earth. Whenever I bring clouds over the earth and the rainbow appears in the clouds, I will remember my covenant between me and you and all living creatures of every kind. Never again will the waters become a flood to destroy all life. Whenever the rainbow appears in the clouds, I will see it and remember the everlasting covenant between God and all living creatures of every kind on the earth."
>
> So God said to Noah, "This is the sign of the covenant I have established between me and all life on the earth." (verses 11–17)

Like the Adamic covenant, the Noahic covenant was unconditional or unilateral. It's important because it shows God's sovereignty over creation and God's good heart overflowing with generosity and grace.

ABRAHAMIC COVENANT

We mentioned the lavish promises of the Abrahamic covenant in chapter 2, where we focused on one divine provision of the covenant: "Whoever curses you I will curse" (Genesis 12:3). Let's quickly review the other aspects of this unilateral agreement. Here are God's words to Abram (as he was then known):

> The LORD had said to Abram, "Go from your country, your people and your father's household to the land I will show you. I will make you into a great nation, and I will bless you; I will make your name great, and you will be a blessing. I will bless those who bless you, and whoever curses you I will curse; and all peoples on earth will be blessed through you." (Genesis 12:1–3)

The birth of Jesus—Immanuel, "God with us"—was the ultimate fulfillment of God's promise to bless "all peoples on earth" through Abraham.

This promise, an unconditional covenant, was reiterated in Genesis 13:14–17; 15:1–7; and 17:1–8. What a gracious act on God's part. At the time, Abraham lived in Harran. His ancestors had "lived beyond the Euphrates River and worshiped other gods" (Joshua 24:2). Nevertheless, God set His affection on Abram. He chose him and announced His unilateral decision to bless him and all who would come from him (Genesis 12:1–3). The agreement included immense individual blessings to Abraham—that he would have descendants and enjoy personal blessings and a great name. But it was much more than that. God would also make Abraham's family into a great nation. And through that nation the Almighty would bless all nations.

Christians see this promise fulfilled in the way that the Jewish people became the conduit of divine revelation through the prophets and apostles. And they see the ultimate blessing—forgiveness of sin, right standing with God, eternal life—as coming through Jesus Christ, the direct descendant of Abraham.

MOSAIC COVENANT

After leading the twelve tribes of Israel out of slavery in Egypt, Moses guided them to Mount Sinai, where God revealed His law and gave Israel its charter as a nation. This extensive legal code outlined how an unholy people might relate to a holy God and how Israel could live righteously in a wicked world. This covenant contained more than six hundred laws, broken down into commandments (Exodus 20:1–17), rules for daily life (Exodus 21:1–23:19), and ordinances for religious practice (Exodus 25:1–31:18).

Israelites cavort around a statue of a golden calf, breaking the first of the Ten Commandments and, overall, the Mosaic covenant.

Like the Edenic covenant, the Mosaic covenant was conditional. It stipulated that obedience would bring gladness and that defiance would bring trouble. When Moses reviewed the law's provisions for the younger generation that was about to inhabit the Promised Land, he expressed it like this: "See, I am setting before you today a blessing and a curse—the blessing if you obey the commands of the

LORD your God that I am giving you today; the curse if you disobey the commands of the LORD your God and turn from the way that I command you today by following other gods, which you have not known" (Deuteronomy 11:26–28).

Moses carries tablets containing the Ten Commandments down Mount Sinai to the waiting Israelites. The people soon break their promise to obey.

"THIS IS WHAT THE LORD SAYS"

One hundred and seventy times in the New International Version we find the phrase "This is what the LORD says"—and that doesn't include other variations of the phrase (for example, "The word of the LORD came to . . ." or "says the LORD" or "The LORD spoke"). We see the Old Testament writing prophets use such phrases repeatedly, because they were not speaking for themselves or in pursuit of their own agendas. They were messengers of God. They were speaking God's words and God's promises.

When God speaks, it is best to pay close attention.

It's worth noting that when Moses first came down from Mount Sinai with this conditional agreement, "the people all responded together, 'We will do everything the LORD has said.' So Moses brought their answer back to the LORD'" (Exodus 19:8).

Of course, it was only a short time later, while Moses was back atop the mountain meeting with God, that the people promptly reneged on their commitment and began worshiping a god of their own making (see Exodus 32).

To a great degree, the Old Testament is series of cycles—the people of God living out déjà vu cycles of sin, judgment, repentance, and blessing . . . sin, judgment, repentance, and blessing.

It helps to read the Mosaic covenant firsthand, paying attention to the predicted divine consequences the Israelites encountered when they failed to live up to their end of the agreement. This covenant teaches us much about the holy character of God and about what it means to be God's "set-apart" people. It makes us thankful for Jesus Christ, who came to earth and fulfilled the Mosaic law completely. He lived the holy life that God demands—and that no other human could or ever did live.

Christians believe that the sacrifices of this old covenant all point to Jesus. He is, as the prophet John the Baptist described Him, "the Lamb of God, who takes away the sin of the world" (John 1:29). He is, as the writer of Hebrews said, our Great High Priest who brings

A mosaic of John baptizing Jesus. It was John the Baptist who publicly identified Jesus as "the Lamb of God."

us to God: "Unlike the other high priests, he does not need to offer sacrifices day after day, first for his own sins, and then for the sins of the people. He sacrificed for their sins once for all when he offered himself" (Hebrews 7:27).

PALESTINIAN COVENANT

The Palestinian covenant, sometimes known as the land covenant, was announced to the people of God by Moses during his final addresses to the nation of Israel.

When all these blessings and curses I have set before you come on you and you take them to heart wherever the Lord your God disperses you among the nations, and when you and your children return to the Lord your God and obey him with all your heart and with all your soul according to everything I command you today, then the Lord your God will restore your fortunes and have compassion on you and gather you again from all the nations where he scattered you. Even if you have been banished to the most distant land under the heavens, from there the Lord your God will gather you and bring you back. He will bring you to the land that belonged to your ancestors, and you will take possession of it. He will make you more prosperous and numerous than your ancestors. The Lord your God will circumcise your hearts and the hearts of your descendants, so that you may love him with all your heart and with all your soul, and live. The Lord your God will put all these curses on your enemies who hate and persecute you. You will again obey the Lord and follow all his commands I am giving you today. Then the Lord your God will make you most prosperous in all the work of your hands and in the fruit of your womb, the young of your livestock and the crops of your land. The Lord will again delight in you and make you prosperous, just as he delighted in your ancestors, if you obey the Lord your God and keep his commands and decrees that are written in this Book of the Law and turn to the Lord your God with all your heart and with all your soul. (Deuteronomy 30:1–10)

The Palestinian covenant is rooted in the Abrahamic covenant. God had promised Abraham and his descendants land—and He reaffirmed this promise on multiple occasions. The Palestinian covenant is regarded as unconditional even though it seems to have conditional elements. Essentially, it's a promise from God (a) to disperse the people of Israel from the Promised Land, scattering them among the nations for rebelling against Him, and (b) to restore the people back to the land one day—regardless of their trust or lack of trust in God.

The Israelites occupied the Promised Land around 1400 BC. Later, because they continued to disobey God's law and disregard God's prophets who were urging them to turn back to God, they were scattered and taken from the land by the Assyrians and Babylonians in 722 and 586 BC respectively. In 538 BC, Cyrus the Great, the Persian king, allowed them to return to the land and rebuild their temple. Some see this momentous, unexpected turn of events as a partial fulfillment of the Palestinian covenant. But in AD 70, Jerusalem was sacked and destroyed by the Romans, once again sending most Jews into exile.

Many today disagree with the idea that ethnic Jews have a true claim to biblical Israel. Here, Palestinian protesters face off with Israeli soldiers in the West Bank.

Amos ends his prophecy with these words: "'I will plant Israel in their own land, never again to be uprooted from the land I have given them,' says the Lord your God" (Amos 9:15). For this reason, many see the creation of the State of Israel in 1948 as prophetically significant, perhaps even setting the stage for the end times.

The Palestinian covenant is significant because of the marvelous things it reveals about our God: His tenacious love for people like us who fail repeatedly to live as He commands, His sovereign ability to work through unlikely people and messy human affairs to accomplish His purposes, and His faithfulness to keep His promises.

DAVIDIC COVENANT

When David had succeeded Saul as king over Israel, when the ark of God had been brought to Jerusalem at last, and when David finally enjoyed rest from all his enemies, God spoke to Nathan the prophet and gave him a message for David:

> "Now then, tell my servant David, 'This is what the Lord Almighty says: I took you from the pasture, from tending the flock, and appointed you ruler over my people Israel. I have been with you wherever you have gone, and I have cut off all your enemies from before you. Now I will make your name great, like the names of the greatest men on earth. And I will provide a place for my people Israel and will plant them so that they can have a home of their own and no longer be disturbed. Wicked people will not oppress them anymore, as they did at the beginning

and have done ever since the time I appointed leaders over my people Israel. I will also give you rest from all your enemies.

The LORD declares to you that the LORD himself will establish a house for you: When your days are over and you rest with your ancestors, I will raise up your offspring to succeed you, your own flesh and blood, and I will establish his kingdom. He is the one who will build a house for my Name, and I will establish the throne of his kingdom forever. I will be his father, and he

will be my son. When he does wrong, I will punish him with a rod wielded by men, with floggings inflicted by human hands. But my love will never be taken away from him, as I took it away from Saul, whom I removed from before you. Your house and your kingdom will endure forever before me; your throne will be established forever.'" (2 Samuel 7:8–16)

David was far from perfect, but he hungered for God's presence in his life. Here, he leads the ark of the covenant to an honored spot in his capital city, Jerusalem.

Though we do not see the word *covenant* in this passage, other verses in scripture call this a covenant (2 Samuel 23:5; Psalm 89:3). In this unconditional covenant, God pledged—as He had done in the Abrahamic covenant—to "provide a place for [His] people Israel . . . so that they can have a home of their own." He also promised David a son who would build a temple—that is, "a house for [His] Name." This promise was clearly fulfilled in the life of Solomon (see 1 Kings 6–7).

Through Nathan, God also promised that this heir's throne would continue forever—even when he did wrong (see 1 Kings 11:34). Finally, Nathan spoke of descendants and a royal kingdom that would be unending.

Christians read Psalm 89—a psalm explicitly about God's dealings with and promises to David—and pay close attention to the unconditional nature of verses 35–37: "Once for all, I have sworn by my holiness—and I will not lie to David—that his line will continue forever and his throne endure before me like the sun; it will be established forever like the moon, the faithful witness in the sky."

Given Luke's affirmation that Jesus was from the family line of David (Luke 1:32–33), Christians see Jesus as the literal and ultimate fulfillment of the Davidic covenant. Some interpret this eternal rule of Christ in a spiritual way—that He rules in the hearts of His followers now. Others, however, await a day in the future when Jesus will return and rule over an everlasting kingdom from Jerusalem (see Zechariah 14).

The Davidic covenant is a great blessing to believers; it demonstrates God's authority over history, His faithfulness in the face of unfaithfulness, and that Jesus will have the final say. He is Lord, and no power can thwart His ultimate reign.

NEW COVENANT

The eighth covenant mentioned in the Old Testament is known as the new covenant. It's found in the prophecies of Jeremiah:

> "The days are coming," declares the LORD, "when I will make a new covenant with the people of Israel and with the people of Judah. It will not be like the covenant I made with their ancestors when I took them by the hand to lead them out of Egypt, because they broke my covenant, though I was a husband to them," declares the LORD. "This is the covenant I will make with the people of Israel after that time," declares the LORD. "I will put my law in their minds and write it on their hearts. I will be their God, and they will be my people. No longer will they teach their neighbor, or say to one another, 'Know the LORD,' because they will all know me, from the least of them to the greatest," declares the LORD. "For I will forgive their wickedness and will remember their sins no more." (Jeremiah 31:31–34)

Under the previous covenants, countless doves, bulls, and sheep were sacrificed for people's sin. But under the new covenant, the Lamb of God—Jesus—provides a single sacrifice for all time.

The Flemish master Peter Paul Rubens (1577–1640) painted *The Elevation of the Cross*, dramatically portraying the once-for-all sacrifice Jesus made for human sin.

Notice that this new covenant was meant to replace the covenant the Israelites previously broke—that is, the Mosaic covenant. It was and is unconditional in nature. God promised the Israelites He would write His law on their hearts. He promised that He would still be their God and that they would still be His people. He also pledged to forgive and forget their sins. In the New Testament, the writer of Hebrews says, "By calling this covenant 'new,' he has made the first one obsolete; and what is obsolete and outdated will soon disappear" (Hebrews 8:13).

Dispensationalists argue that the ultimate fulfillment of this new covenant must still be in the future because, at present, not all Jewish people know the Lord in a personal way. They add that it is still necessary to teach the truth of God to the millions who lack a correct understanding of God. Other scholars concede that this promise was first made to Israel; however, they say it is now available to everyone who trusts Jesus Christ as Savior (Matthew 26:28; Hebrews 9:15).

The writer of Hebrews spent a great deal of time comparing the old Mosaic covenant with the new covenant. The writer indicated that the old system of law was given to highlight the need for the new covenant. The Mosaic law showed two things: (1) God's perfect standard of righteousness and (2) humanity's inability to live up to that standard. Whereas the old (Mosaic) covenant was made exclusively with Israel, the blessings of the new covenant are available to Israel and Gentiles (see Hebrews 8).

Such blessing is hard to fathom. The old Mosaic covenant required an army of imperfect priests. The new covenant features one perfect High Priest. The Mosaic covenant called for endless sacrifices. The new covenant required one final and sufficient sacrifice: "Christ . . . has appeared once for all atthe culmination of the ages to do away with sin by the sacrifice of himself" (Hebrews 9:26). The Mosaic covenant involved trying in vain to live out laws chiseled into cold stone. The new covenant involves God changing our hearts by filling them with His truth.

These eight biblical covenants tell the story of God's dealings with people. The Edenic and Adamic and Noahic covenants show God's interactions with the whole world. The Abrahamic, Mosaic, Palestinian, Davidic, and new covenants show how God has worked in and through the nation of Israel to regain the paradise that was lost in the fall.

Many aspects of these grand and glorious covenants have already come to pass. In other ways, we are still seeing or awaiting their fulfillment. As such, these eight binding agreements form the foundation for all biblical prophecy. Careful study of them can guide us as we seek to interpret and understand prophecy.

A man from the group Jews for Jesus hands out flyers on the streets of Tel Aviv, Israel. The organization's mission is to "relentlessly pursue God's plan for the salvation of the Jewish people."

Chapter 5:
PROPHECIES BY DANIEL

If you've ever been in a *really* dark place—for example, battling chronic pain, facing a dire medical prognosis, fretting over a rebellious and self-destructive child, feeling trapped in a dead-end, low-paying job—you know firsthand what it's like to wonder if things will *ever* take a positive turn.

Some 2,500 years ago, the people of Judah found themselves in a helpless, hopeless situation. Their country had been overrun by the fierce Babylonians. In 586 BC, their brightest and best had been forced into exile. Suddenly they were captives in a foreign country working for a godless government. Would they ever see their

The angel Gabriel carried God's messages to Daniel, who recorded them for future generations.

homeland again? Had the God of their fathers Abraham and Moses and David abandoned them?

Thankfully, for them—and for us—the prophet Daniel was God's man "on the ground" during that grim time. In God's merciful plan, He had Daniel write down on parchment all sorts of prophecies to encourage the Jewish people to hope in God—to wait with confident expectation that God was at work in history, weaving all things together for His glory and their good.

Many of Daniel's vivid and dramatic prophecies were fulfilled in his lifetime. We'll look at those supernatural predictions in this chapter. He prophesied the rise and fall of the world's dominant powers. Some scholars even believe he predicted the exact year of Jesus' death.

At the same time, many of Daniel's most compelling and detailed visions are yet to be fulfilled. We'll explore them in a later chapter. It's no wonder that both Bible students and prophecy experts are fascinated by this ancient record that combines gripping stories of brave, young men with cryptic visions of the future.

WHO WAS DANIEL?

We know almost nothing about Daniel's early life, except that he was of the Jewish noble class (Daniel 1:3). He was likely just a teenager when King Nebuchadnezzar deported him to Babylon. Upon arriving in his new home, he and the others were immediately placed in a three-year training program for royal service. They learned the Babylonian language and culture (Daniel 1:4). Because of their intelligence, integrity, and devotion to the law of their God, Daniel (renamed Belteshazzar) and his three friends Hananiah, Mishael, and Azariah (renamed Shadrach, Meshach, and Abednego) quickly distinguished themselves. At the end of their training, the four were presented to Nebuchadnezzar; and "in every matter of wisdom and understanding about which the king questioned them, he found them ten times better than all the magicians and enchanters in his whole kingdom" (Daniel 1:20).

Daniel served with distinction as a royal advisor for decades, "until the first year of King Cyrus" (Daniel 1:21). He survived the fall of the Babylonian Empire, and he kept his prestigious position when Darius the Mede rose to power (Daniel 5:30–31).

Though he is probably best known for surviving a night in a lions' den, Daniel was also a prolific prophet who described "the time of the end" (Daniel 8:17) as announced by the angel Gabriel.

Daniel is perhaps best known for being thrown into the lions' den (see Daniel 6). It happened like this: Daniel's Chaldean colleagues were envious of his great influence and high position. So they tried desperately but without success to find a "skeleton in his closet" that they might use to take him down. When his "closet" was free of even the hint of scandal, Daniel's enemies tried a different tack. Knowing that Daniel was fiercely devoted to his God, they convinced the king to impulsively sign off on a new law forbidding prayer to anyone but Darius, under penalty of death.

Daniel was unfazed and undaunted by this edict. He continued his practice of praying three times daily in front of an open window that faced Jerusalem. As a result, he was promptly arrested. Darius was distraught when he realized what he had done; he was beside himself with grief. However, he had rubber-stamped the anti-prayer law, and it didn't contain any loopholes. Ironically, as he reluctantly ordered his men to toss Daniel into the lions' den for praying to the God of the Hebrews, he uttered a kind of prayer himself: "May your God, whom you serve continually, rescue you!" (Daniel 6:16).

God heard and God answered. The Lord shut the mouths of the lions. In one of the greatest plot twists ever, Darius then fed the framers of the law to the lions. Lastly, he issued a new decree—that everyone in his kingdom "must fear and reverence the God of Daniel" (Daniel 6:26).

Daniel's life inspires us to hope. So do his prophecies. In and through it all, we see a God who is faithful, merciful, and in control of all things.

A common impression of "the apocalypse." While the Bible does describe frightening events in the future, it also provides hope and comfort through Jesus Christ.

WHAT IS APOCALYPTIC LITERATURE?

The book of Daniel is regarded as a special kind of prophetic writing known as apocalyptic literature. This genre became popular after the Jewish exile and was widely utilized through the first century. The term comes from the Greek word *apokalypsis*, which means "unveiling" or "uncovering." Such divine messages are typically given through visions or dreams—and often include angelic visitation. The visions are often full of bewildering images and figurative language. The idea is that without a supernatural "pulling back of the curtains," future events could not be known in advance.

This kind of prophetic writing focuses heavily on eschatolo ical elements—things having to do with the end of the world. It a

1

INTERPRETING APOCALYPTIC LITERATURE

When studying apocalyptic literature, it's important to **note the heavy use of symbolism**. Because apocalyptic literature includes so much symbolic imagery, we have to approach books like Daniel differently than we would approach, say, the Gospel of John. For example, at the end of his Gospel, John wrote: "When the soldiers crucified Jesus, they took his clothes, dividing them into four shares, one for each of them" (John 19:23). Because this is narrative literature, it's reasonable to assume that John meant Jesus' garments were divided into four literal parts. However, when Daniel wrote about seeing "a lion, and it had the wings of an eagle" (Daniel 7:4), no one expected such a creature to materialize in human history. In apocalyptic literature, colors and objects are often meant to represent attributes of something; for example, white signifies purity. Grasping the symbolic nature of apocalyptic literature helps us understand it.

This does not mean, of course, that there is nothing literal about apocalyptic literature. The reason this genre is so difficult to interpret is because it contains both literal and symbolic elements. For example, how do we interpret Daniel 7:9–10, which says that "the books were opened" in front of "the Ancient of Days" who was seated on a "throne . . . flaming with fire"? Is God's throne really on fire? Are there actual books—as we think of books—in heaven? Or do these descriptions suggest other truths, perhaps God's holiness and perfect justice? The student of the Word needs to wrestle with these things, and not everyone will arrive at the same conclusions.

focuses on the resurrection of the dead and features a strong messianic hope. Biblical apocalyptic literature includes the books of Daniel and Revelation. This kind of vivid writing is also seen in Isaiah 24–27; 33–35; Jeremiah 33:14–26; Ezekiel 38–39; Joel 3:9–17; Zechariah 12–14; Matthew 24; Mark 13; and 2 Thessalonians 2.

Let's take a peek now at some of Daniel's apocalyptic dreams and visions that were fulfilled either in his lifetime or in subsequent centuries.

DANIEL THE DREAMER (AND DREAM INTERPRETER)

In Daniel 2, we find the story of a troubled Babylonian king, Nebuchadnezzar, having a disturbing dream and not being able to sleep. The narrative tells us that the king promptly summoned his "magicians, enchanters, sorcerers and astrologers" (Daniel 2:1–11) and ordered them to tell him not just the meaning of his dream but the dream itself. When this retinue of "wise men" protested, the agitated king ordered his guards to execute the whole lot of them. Cue the young Daniel to courageously intervene.

Young Daniel appears before the mighty Nebuchadnezzar, giving God full credit for his ability to interpret the king's dream.

Daniel humbly asked the king for some time "so that he might interpret the dream for him" (Daniel 2:16). After praying with his friends (2:17–23), Daniel told the king, "There is a God in heaven who reveals mysteries" (2:28).

Daniel told the king how the dream had begun. He told him about seeing "an enormous, dazzling statue, awesome in appearance. The head of the statue was made of pure gold, its chest and arms of silver, its belly and thighs of bronze, its legs of iron, its feet partly of iron and partly of baked clay" (Daniel 2:31–33).

Then Daniel told the king how the dream had ended: "While you were watching, a rock was cut out, but not by human hands. It struck the statue on its feet of iron and clay and smashed them. Then the iron, the clay, the bronze, the silver and the gold were all broken to pieces and became like chaff on a threshing floor in the summer. The wind swept them away without leaving a trace. But the rock

113

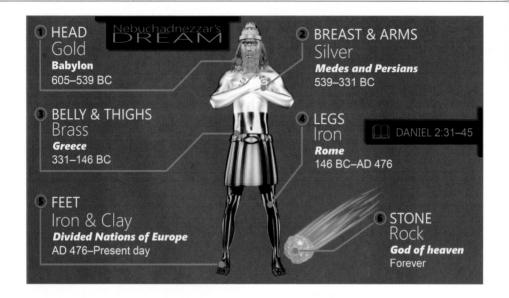

that struck the statue became a huge mountain and filled the whole earth" (Daniel 2:34–35).

Finally, Daniel conveyed the meaning of the dream. He told Nebuchadnezzar, "You are that head of gold" (Daniel 2:38), and he prophesied that the king and his kingdom would be succeeded by an inferior kingdom. "Next, a third kingdom, one of bronze, will rule over the whole earth" (Daniel 2:39). Daniel spoke of a fourth kingdom, which many prophecy experts interpret as Rome. Others see the possibility of two distinct "Roman Empires," the one we know from history, and a revived version during the end times.

Here is what we can say for sure: In Daniel 8:20–21, those first two kingdoms of Nebuchadnezzar's dream are clearly identified as Medo-Persia and Greece. History shows the fulfillment of Daniel's two-part prophecy in the rise of the Medo-Persian Empire in 539 BC and, subsequently, in Alexander the Great's rise to power in 323 BC.

In Daniel 4, King Nebuchadnezzar was once again having wild dreams. Skeptics might cite the old urban legend that says eating too much spicy food late at night is what causes this phenomenon.

We know the truth. God was speaking. Nebuchadnezzar summoned Daniel and told him about seeing a huge and beautiful and fruitful tree.

Next he described hearing a messenger from heaven call out, "Cut down the tree and trim off its branches; strip off its leaves and scatter its fruit. Let the animals flee from under it and the birds from its branches. But let the stump and its roots, bound with iron and bronze, remain in the ground, in the grass of the field" (Daniel 4:14–15).

INTERPRETING APOCALYPTIC LITERATURE

When studying apocalyptic literature, it's important to **note the writer's vantage point**. As players in the unfolding human drama, we naturally tend to view history horizontally and sequentially. God, the author and director of the great story in which we find ourselves, has a radically different perspective. Outside of the constraints of time, He sees the beginning, middle, and end. Indeed, He has a thirty-thousand-foot view of reality.

When reading apocalyptic literature, it's crucial to remember that God enabled the writers to see from His standpoint, not a human one. This means we get to see human history—and humanity's future—from a heavenly perspective. The book of Daniel challenges us in this respect, giving us a glimpse of God seated on His heavenly throne, judgments being poured out on those who defy Him, and the books—including, presumably, the book of life (Revelation 3:5)—being opened (see Daniel 7:9–10).

Scholars are quick to note that apocalyptic imagery can sometimes stretch over more than one period of history, or jump backward and forward in time. In *An Approach to Apocalyptic Literature: A Primer for Preachers*, David R. Helm refers to this as the "elasticity of vantage point."[1]

The saying "you can't see the forest for the trees" means human beings often lack the big-picture perspective they need— the perspective God has at all times.

Nebuchadnezzar told Daniel that the messenger in the dream then switched metaphors. He stopped speaking of a tree and seemed to refer to a man. "Let him be drenched with the dew of heaven, and let him live with the animals among the plants of the earth. Let his mind be changed from that of a man and let him be given the mind of an animal, till seven times pass by for him" (Daniel 4:15–16).

The king, his voice no doubt shaking with fear, then pleaded with Daniel, "This is the dream that I, King Nebuchadnezzar, had. Now, Belteshazzar, tell me what it means, for none of the wise men in my kingdom can interpret it for me. But you can, because the spirit of the holy gods is in you" (Daniel 4:18).

With great courage and tact, Daniel informed the king, "Your Majesty, you are that tree! You have become great and strong; your greatness has grown until it reaches the sky, and your dominion extends to distant parts of the earth" (Daniel 4:22).

There might have been a long pause, and perhaps a gulp, before Daniel told Nebuchadnezzar the rest of the unpleasant truth. "You will be driven away from people and will live with the wild animals; you will eat grass like the ox and be drenched with the dew of heaven. Seven times will pass by for you until you acknowledge that the Most High is sovereign over all kingdoms on earth and gives them to anyone he wishes" (Daniel 4:25).

As only a true prophet could or would, Daniel then seized on the opportunity to urge the king to repent: "Therefore, Your Majesty, be pleased to accept my advice: Renounce your sins by doing what is right, and your wickedness by being kind to the oppressed. It may be that then your prosperity will continue" (Daniel 4:27).

The king would not repent. Daniel 4:28–37 records how Nebuchadnezzar's pride got the best of him. Twelve months later, as the king was boastfully admiring his kingdom, "immediately what had

Nebuchadnezzar is not a pretty sight in this late eighteenth-century painting by William Blake. But the reality of this quickly fulfilled prophecy may have been even worse.

been said about Nebuchadnezzar was fulfilled. He was driven away from people and ate grass like the ox. His body was drenched with the dew of heaven until his hair grew like the feathers of an eagle and his nails like the claws of a bird" (Daniel 4:33).

For seven years Nebuchadnezzar lived the bovine life. Medical experts identify this condition in which people act like oxen as *boanthropy*, or *insania zoanthropica*. Only when he humbled himself before God was King Nebuchadnezzar restored.

In Daniel 5 we find another prophecy and another fulfillment. This chapter tells of a great feast hosted by King Belshazzar, the son of Nebuchadnezzar. In the drunken revelry of this pagan party,

Belshazzar told his servants to fetch the silver and gold goblets that had been seized out of the temple in Jerusalem. These holy implements were then used by the king and his guests to make toasts to Bel and to other gods worshiped by the Babylonians—and to mock Yahweh, the God of the Israelites.

Daniel recorded what happened next. "Suddenly the fingers of a human hand appeared and wrote on the plaster of the wall, near the lampstand in the royal palace. The king watched the hand as it wrote. His face turned pale and he was so frightened that his legs became weak and his knees were knocking" (Daniel 5:5–6).

King Belshazzar and his party guests are shocked by the hand writing on the wall—another biblical prophecy that was fulfilled very quickly.

The king's diviners and astrologers were quickly summoned. Looking at the message, they could only scratch their heads. The queen entered the banquet hall. She reminded the terrified king of how the foreigner Daniel had often helped Nebuchadnezzar in such puzzling situations. She described Daniel as having "a keen mind and knowledge and understanding, and also the ability to interpret dreams, explain riddles and solve difficult problems." With urgency she said, "Call for Daniel, and he will tell you what the writing means" (Daniel 5:12).

When the courtly Daniel arrived—probably close to age eighty by this time—he was apprised of the situation. With a gentle boldness, the venerable old prophet reminded everyone of what had happened when Nebuchadnezzar got too big for his kingly britches—how he'd spent seven years grazing on grass in solitude. With courage and firmness, the prophet continued: "But you, Belshazzar, his son, have not humbled yourself, though you knew all this" (Daniel 5:22).

Daniel finished up by interpreting the strange words that had been scrawled on the wall: *Mene, Mene, Tekel, Parsin*. The meaning, in essence: "Your reign has come to an end. The Medes and Persians will now split your kingdom."

Did this prophecy come to pass? Absolutely and immediately.

"That very night Belshazzar, king of the Babylonians, was slain, and Darius the Mede took over the kingdom, at the age of sixty-two" (Daniel 5:30–31).

119

In Daniel 7 we read about one of the prophet's stranger visions. The chapter begins with these words: "In the first year of Belshazzar king of Babylon, Daniel had a dream, and visions passed through his mind as he was lying in bed. He wrote down the substance of his dream" (Daniel 7:1).

This would have been around 553–550 BC, more than ten years prior to the events we just looked at in Daniel 5.

In this vision, Daniel saw four beasts rising up out of the sea. The first looked like a lion with eagles' wings. Daniel wrote, "I watched until its wings were torn off and it was lifted from the ground so that it stood on two feet like a human being, and the mind of a human was given to it" (Daniel 7:4).

The second beast looked like a bear. Daniel reported that it "had three ribs in its mouth between its teeth. It was told, 'Get up and eat your fill of flesh!'" (Daniel 7:5).

The third beast looked like a four-headed leopard with four wings of a bird; this beast was "given authority to rule" (Daniel 7:6).

INTERPRETING APOCALYPTIC LITERATURE

When studying apocalyptic literature, it's important to **note repetitive themes**. Often in apocalyptic literature certain terms or themes are used repeatedly to give structure to the whole work. A vivid example is John's use of the number seven in Revelation. In biblical literature, the number seven represents completeness or perfection. John mentions seven letters addressed to seven churches (Revelation 2–3). This is followed by a description of a scroll with seven seals (Revelation 5:1–8:5). After the seven seals come seven trumpets (8:6–11:19). Then John reports seven visions (12:1–15:4), followed by a vivid description of seven bowls of divine judgment (15:5–18:24). One thought is that John was using the number seven repeatedly to emphasize that God's plan, for both His people and the world, is perfect.

Some prophetic imagery is hard to imagine. Here is nineteenth-century engraver Gustave Doré's attempt to depict Daniel's four beasts from the sea.

Daniel wrote that the fourth beast was "terrifying and frightening and very powerful. It had large iron teeth; it crushed and devoured its victims and trampled underfoot whatever was left. It was different from all the former beasts, and it had ten horns" (Daniel 7:7).

After this, Daniel reported having seen a smaller horn spring up among the others and speak boastfully. Then, suddenly, the vision shifted into something resembling a court setting. Daniel saw one he called the "Ancient of Days" sitting on a blazing throne. This one with hair white as wool then acted as a judge as "ten thousand times ten thousand stood before him" (Daniel 7:9–10).

The vision ended with Daniel saying, "Before me was one like a son of man, coming with the clouds of heaven. He approached the

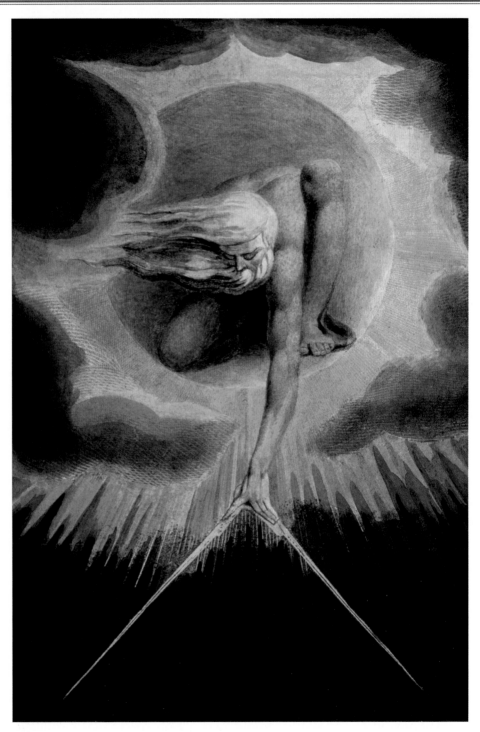

William Blake's 1794 painting *Ancient of Days*.

Ancient of Days and was led into his presence. He was given authority, glory and sovereign power; all nations and peoples of every language worshiped him. His dominion is an everlasting dominion that will not pass away, and his kingdom is one that will never be destroyed" (Daniel 7:13–14).

What do we make of such visions?

Interpreters have all sorts of ideas about what this vivid imagery might mean. Perhaps, one group surmises, this is a prophecy that was fulfilled partly in the past and that will receive its ultimate fulfillment in the future. If so, this would be a good example of prophetic telescoping.

In this view, the first beast represents Babylon—specifically Nebuchadnezzar being humbled and then receiving back his mind. The second beast represents Medo-Persia, which defeated Babylonia in 539 BC. Daniel 8:20–22 explicitly identifies the Medo-Persian and Greek Empires, although in that prophecy the imagery is different. The Daniel 8 vision features a ram and a goat, not the strange beasts we see in Daniel 7.

The third beast is said to be Greece under Alexander the Great. Like a leopard, his rise to power was speedy. Interpreters point out that when he died in 323 BC, his kingdom was split among four generals—Lysimachus, Cassander, Seleucus, and Ptolemy. This would certainly seem to correspond to the creature in the vision having four heads and four wings.

What about the fourth beast? Daniel seemed to be particularly troubled by this part of his vision (see Daniel 7:15–20). Some argue that the historic Roman Empire seems to fit the description.

The third beast of Daniel's vision looked like a leopard, but with four heads and wings.

Others, however, point to what the angel told Daniel: "The fourth beast . . . will be different from all the other kingdoms and will devour the whole earth, trampling it down and crushing it" (Daniel 7:23). As far-reaching as the ancient Roman Empire was, the argument goes, it did not encompass "the whole earth." This leads many to conclude that the final fulfillment of this prophecy—the rise of the fourth beast—is yet future.

In Daniel 8 we find another vision, this one from the third year of Belshazzar's reign in about 550 BC. Daniel saw a ram doing whatever it pleased, until it was overpowered by a shaggy male goat. The angel Gabriel explained, "The two-horned ram that you saw represents the kings of Media and Persia. The shaggy goat is the king of Greece, and the large horn between its eyes is the first king" (Daniel 8:20–21).

Historians tell us that the Medes and Persians conquered Babylon in 539 BC. They were the world superpower for two centuries until Alexander the Great led the Greek armies on a whirlwind campaign to try to conquer the world.

Daniel's next vision included an aggressive, shaggy goat that the angel Gabriel described as the king of Greece.

Daniel wasn't through prophesying. Around 538 BC Daniel wrote that he was reading the prophecies of Jeremiah that describe the Jews serving the king of Babylon for seventy years (Daniel 9:1–2; see Jeremiah 25:11–12; 29:10–14). Looking at the calendar, Daniel realized that the time of the exile must be drawing to a close. While praying and fasting about this, Daniel received a visit from the angel Gabriel, who gave him the famous prophecy of "seventy weeks," one of the most stirring and complicated prophecies in the Bible.

It begins with these words: "Seventy 'sevens' are decreed for your people and your holy city to finish transgression, to put an end to sin, to atone for wickedness, to bring in everlasting righteousness, to seal up vision and prophecy and to anoint the Most Holy Place" (Daniel 9:24).

While some interpret these cryptic numbers to mean simply "a long time," most see them in a different way. They believe a "seven" is actually a seven-year period. If correct, the seventy "sevens" refer to seventy "weeks" of years, or 490 years. This vision, therefore, acts as a cryptic, prophetic clock.

In the next verse, the angel divided the 490 years into two smaller units of time. He said that "from the time the word goes out to restore and rebuild Jerusalem until the Anointed One, the ruler, comes," there would be one period of seven "sevens" (forty-nine years) and another of sixty-two "sevens" (434 years). That's a combined 483 years.

Now consider this: in late 445 or early 444 BC, King Artaxerxes authorized Nehemiah to return to Jerusalem and rebuild the city's walls. Did this start the clock ticking on Daniel's prophecy? Many scholars think so. If we consider the fact that many ancient calendars had 360 days—not 365 days—and then do a little math (444 BC plus

Many believe Daniel's prophecy of the "seventy sevens" pinpointed the time of Jesus' crucifixion.

483 years), we arrive at about AD 30. Many consider this to be the year of Jesus' crucifixion. If this interpretation is correct, then Jesus' death was the fulfillment of Daniel's prophecy, that when 483 years are completed, the "Anointed One will be put to death" (Daniel 9:26).

If all the above is valid, then sixty-nine of the seventy "sevens" have already been fulfilled, leaving one more "seven." Some believe we are living in a gap between the sixty-ninth and seventieth weeks. If so, it's as if God's prophetic clock has been paused. What about that seventieth week? We'll discuss that in a future chapter.

Daniel's prophecy can be extremely confusing, but Christians can rejoice in the truth that God is the Lord of history. He knows the "end from the beginning" (Isaiah 46:10), and He is sovereign over all the details.

We probably need to mention a controversial prophecy found in Daniel 8:9–14. Some say it has been fulfilled in history; others disagree. It involves a small horn coming forth from the goat, the Greek Empire. This horn is said to grow in power "to the south and to the east and toward the Beautiful Land" (Daniel 8:9). Daniel wrote, "It took away the daily sacrifice from the LORD, and his sanctuary was thrown down" (Daniel 8:11).

Many conservative scholars see this prophecy fulfilled in the reign of Antiochus IV—also known as Antiochus Epiphanes, which means "god manifest"—in 175–164 BC. Remember how Alexander's kingdom was divided by his top generals upon his death? Seleucus was one of those four generals, and he established a dynasty that ruled over Syria, Mesopotamia, and Asia Minor. Antiochus IV was the eighth of the Seleucid rulers, and he is regarded as one of the most vicious rulers ever. A devotee of Zeus, he did his best to Hellenize his subjects— that is, to get them to embrace Greek culture

A bust of Antiochus Epiphanes, on display in the Altes Museum, Berlin, Germany.

and religion. The Jews in Judah fiercely resisted his attempts to "convert" them, and so he took draconian measures, forbidding every sort of Jewish religious expression. He even defiled the Jerusalem temple by offering sacrifices of swine to Greek gods on its altar. In these horrific acts, many see the fulfillment of the phrase "the rebellion that causes desolation" (Daniel 8:13) or, as it is expressed in Daniel 11:31, "the abomination that causes desolation."

In Daniel 11, we find what theologian John Walvoord called "the most detailed prophecy to be found anywhere in Scripture."[2] It's a foretelling of key events and significant rulers that would follow the rule of Darius, ending with a vision of the evil Antiochus.

Daniel spoke of a powerful Persian king who would "stir up everyone against the kingdom of Greece" (Daniel 11:2). In history this would have been Xerxes I, who attacked Greece around 480 BC—some fifty years after Daniel's death. A subsequent king would "do as the pleases," and his empire would be "broken up and parceled out to the four winds of heaven" (Daniel 11:3–4). These are clear references to Alexander the Great. On and on Daniel goes, giving startling details of coming events. His prophetic declarations are aligned with the documented historical squabbling and interactions between the four kingdoms spawned from Alexander's death.

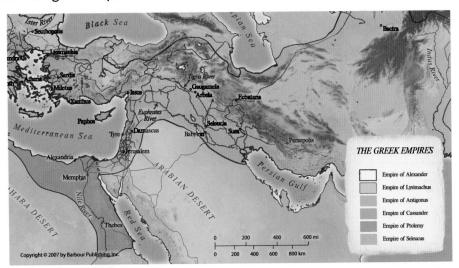

ABOMINATION OF DESOLATION

An abomination is something detestable (Genesis 46:34). In the Old Testament, the word is used to describe the worship of idols in particular (2 Kings 23:13; Jeremiah 44:4), and sinful acts in general (Isaiah 66:3). The phrase "abomination that causes desolation" comes from Daniel 11:31 and 12:11.

Many see this cryptic announcement fulfilled in the despicable acts of Antiochus. In Luke 21:20, Jesus referred to a coming "desolation," perhaps alluding to the Roman troops that would destroy Jerusalem and the temple in AD 70. Some conservative scholars think that this phrase also points to events that will happen at the end of the world when one called the Antichrist moves against God's holy city.

It's easy to see how Daniel's prophecies, complicated though they are, would have brought relief to Jewish exiles who were feeling hopeless in Babylon. As we live in a day of immense global tension and personal uncertainty, Daniel's words are a great comfort to us as well. Especially encouraging are the final words of his book:

> I heard, but I did not understand. So I asked, "My lord, what will the outcome of all this be?" He replied, "Go your way, Daniel, because the words are rolled up and sealed until the time of the end. Many will be purified, made spotless and refined, but the wicked will continue to be wicked. None of the wicked will understand, but those who are wise will understand. . . . As for you, go your way till the end. You will rest, and then at the end of the days you will rise to receive your allotted inheritance." (Daniel 12:8–10, 13)

Endnotes

1   David R. Helm, *An Approach to Apocalyptic Literature: A Primer for Preachers* (Chicago: The Simeon Trust, 2009), 14.
2   John Walvoord, *The Prophecy Knowledge Handbook* (Dallas Seminary Press, 1990), 263.

Chapter 6:

BIBLICAL PROPHECIES ABOUT JESUS CHRIST

One of the most intriguing stories from the life of Jesus is found at the end of the Gospel of Luke.

On a solemn Sunday afternoon, two disheartened followers of Jesus were trudging from Jerusalem to the village of Emmaus, some seven miles away. They were talking about all the confusing, tumultuous events of the last few days: the throngs of people who cheered Jesus the previous Sunday; the intense debates between their teacher and the Jewish religious leaders in the temple courts; the arrest of

Cleopas and his companion unwittingly talk with the resurrected Jesus on the road to Emmaus.

Jesus on Thursday night; the bloodthirsty mob calling for His execution early Friday morning; the horrors of the crucifixion.

"As they talked and discussed these things with each other, Jesus himself came up and walked along with them; but they were kept from recognizing him. He asked them, 'What are you discussing together as you walk along?'" (Luke 24:15–17).

The men stopped in their tracks. Glumly, and maybe with a bit of irritation, the one named Cleopas replied, "Are you the only one visiting Jerusalem who does not know the things that have happened there in these days?" (Luke 24:18).

Perhaps stifling a smile, Jesus played dumb. "What things?" He asked (Luke 24:19).

The men proceeded to tell Jesus all about Jesus: the marvelous things He'd said and done, the terrible things done to Him over the weekend. And they reported the latest rumor racing through the grapevine, that Jesus' tomb was *empty*.

Jesus' response to the men is remarkable and worth our careful attention: "'How foolish you are, and how slow to believe *all that the prophets have spoken*! Did not the Messiah have to suffer these things and then enter his glory?' *And beginning with Moses and all the*

Prophets, he explained to them what was said in all the Scriptures concerning himself" (Luke 24:25–27, emphasis added).

It's important to grasp what Christ was claiming in this moment. He was saying, "Friends, I am not *a* theme of the Bible; I am *the* theme. From beginning to end, the holy scriptures and all those ancient prophecies point to *me!*"

This is what Christianity teaches: The whole Old Testament anticipates the coming of a Messiah; the entire New Testament introduces and celebrates Jesus of Nazareth as that promised Messiah.

"I know that Messiah...is coming," a Samaritan woman told Jesus by a water well. "I, the one speaking to you," Jesus answered, "am he" (John 4:25–26).

Would it be possible to have a book about Bible prophecy without a sizable chapter on all the biblical prophecies pertaining to the coming of Jesus? Not at all.

Like the two disciples on the road to Emmaus, many people are shocked to learn that numerous ancient prophecies about Christ (some have counted more than three hundred) are woven throughout the Old Testament. They include all sorts of detailed predictions about His birth, death, and resurrection, as well as vivid descriptions of His nature and ministry. If you've ever doubted the Bible or the claims of Jesus, you owe it to yourself to read the next few pages prayerfully and carefully.

Let's begin by defining some terms.

THE MEANING OF *MESSIAH*

Our English word *Messiah* comes from the Hebrew word *mashiach*, which means "anointed." The New Testament Greek word for "anointed" is *christos*, or, in English, *Christ*. *Messiah* and *Christ* are synonymous. When we speak of Jesus Christ, we are saying Jesus the Messiah. *Christ* is a title, not a last name.

In the Old Testament, the formal ritual of anointing a leader (Exodus 30:30; 1 Samuel 9:16) with oil was a way of symbolically marking a person as chosen by God for a special task. Prophets, priests, and kings were anointed in a ceremonial way (Exodus 29:7; 1 Kings 19:16) thereby consecrating them, or setting them apart, for a holy calling.

The title *messiah* ("Anointed One") is found in the Old Testament only in Daniel 9:25–26. But the Old Testament is filled with references to a coming person described as a servant, king, savior, and heir of David. Isaiah, for example, includes four "servant songs" (Isaiah 42:1–7; 49:1–9; 50:4–11; 52:13–53:12).

The book of Psalms is brimming with messianic prophecies. Most scholars see *at least* twenty predictions of Christ that they argue were fulfilled in the life of Jesus: Psalms 2:7; 8:6; 16:10; 22:1; 22:7–8; 22:16; 22:18; 31:5; 34:20; 35:19; 40:7–8; 41:9; 45:6; 68:18; 69:9; 69:21; 110:1; 110:4; 118:22; 118:26. Others see far more. Some see still other messianic prophecies in Psalms that they believe are yet to be fulfilled (Psalms 72:7–11, 17–19; 96:13; 132:3–18).

The covenant God made with King David included the unconditional promise that his kingdom would be unending. But David's kingdom sputtered and then split after Solomon's reign. The Assyrians

In a sixteenth-century painting by Paolo Veronese, the prophet Samuel pours oil for the anointing of the young shepherd David as Israel's next king.

invaded in 722 BC, scattering the ten northern tribes. In 586 BC, the Babylonians took the people of Judah and Jerusalem into exile. From that time forward, Jewish hopes for an anointed king and deliverer only increased. They never diminished.

THE MESSIAH AND THE PSALMS

As with the prophecies in other sections of scripture, not everyone agrees on how to interpret all the messianic mentions in Psalms. Some, believing that the psalms primarily speak about events in the lives of the writers, argue that any messianic tones—real or imagined—are merely coincidental. Others theorize that the psalmists were prophesying without realizing it.

Whatever their *intent*, it is obvious from the psalmists' *writings* that they viewed God as both patient and faithful to His people. They clearly expected that by His sovereign power He would one day redeem His people and make good on all His promises.

Most Jews do not believe that Jesus is the Messiah the scriptures promised. Messianic Jews however, are ethnic Jews who do accept the claims of Jesus Christ in the New Testament.

WHAT IS MESSIANIC PROPHECY?

Messianic prophecy is any divine announcement delivered by an authorized prophet of God concerning the predicted king-priest from the family line of David, the One who would be anointed by God to rescue God's people and carry out God's ultimate purposes on the earth.

With this understanding of *messiah* and *messianic prophecy,* let's look at just a few of the hundreds of Old Testament prophecies concerning Christ that Christians believe were fulfilled during the life of Jesus on earth.

PROPHECIES ABOUT THE MESSIAH'S LINEAGE AND BIRTH

The Messiah would be a descendant of Jacob. The non-Israelite prophet Balaam said, "I see him, but not now; I behold him, but not near. A star will come out of Jacob; a scepter will rise out of Israel. He will crush the foreheads of Moab, the skulls of all the people of Sheth" (Numbers 24:17).

In the extensive genealogy found in Luke 3, Jacob is listed as an ancestor of Jesus (verse 34).

The Messiah would be from the Israelite tribe of Judah. Micah singled out the Israelite tribe from which the Messiah would arise: "But you, Bethlehem Ephrathah, though you are small among the clans of Judah, out of you will come for me one who will be ruler over Israel, whose origins are from of old, from ancient times" (Micah 5:2).

Judah is listed as an ancestor of Jesus in Luke 3:33.

The modern city of Bethlehem. Just a small town in Jesus' time, Bethlehem had been prophesied as His birthplace centuries earlier.

The Messiah would come from the line of Jesse. Isaiah gave even more precise details about the Messiah's origins. "A shoot will come up from the stump of Jesse; from his roots a Branch will bear fruit" (Isaiah 11:1).

Jesse is listed as an ancestor of Jesus in Luke 3:32.

The Messiah would come from the house of David. Jesse had multiple sons. Jeremiah made it clear which of these sons would head the messianic line: "'The days are coming' declares the LORD, 'when I will raise up *for David* a righteous Branch, a King who will reign wisely and do what is just and right in the land'" (Jeremiah 23:5, emphasis added).

Sure enough, David is listed as an ancestor of Jesus in Luke 3:31.

The Messiah would be the Son of God. God, speaking through the prophet Nathan, essentially told David, "Your son will be my Son." Many see this as an overt claim

The baptism of Jesus as envisioned by the nineteenth-century lithographers Currier and Ives. As Jesus came up from the water, the Holy Spirit appeared like a dove, and God's voice announced, "This is my Son, whom I love" (Matthew 3:17).

that the Messiah would be divine. The exact words of the prophecy? "I will be his father, and he will be my son. I will never take my love away from him, as I took it away from your predecessor. I will set him over my house and my kingdom forever; his throne will be established forever" (1 Chronicles 17:13–14).

Consider that at the baptism of Jesus, a voice from heaven announced, "This is my Son, whom I love; with him I am well pleased" (Matthew 3:17).

The Messiah would come as a newborn. Isaiah shared this glorious announcement with Israel: "For to us a child is born, to us a son is given, and the government will be on his shoulders. And he will be called Wonderful Counselor, Mighty God, Everlasting Father, Prince of Peace" (Isaiah 9:6).

On the night Jesus was born, an angel announced to some shepherds who were tending their flocks near Bethlehem, "Today in the town of David a Savior has been born to you; he is the Messiah, the Lord" (Luke 2:11).

The Messiah would be born of a virgin. One of the best-known messages given to the prophet Isaiah involved a virgin having a baby: "Therefore the Lord himself will give you a sign: The virgin will conceive and give birth to a son, and will call him Immanuel" (Isaiah 7:14).

Bible interpreters often argue over this prophecy because of the ambiguous Hebrew word *'almah*, which is translated *virgin* in our

The Bible never gives Mary's age, but the implication is that she was young. Luke's Gospel is careful to specify her status as a virgin (1:34).

English Bibles. It simply means "a young woman of marriageable age." In other words, it can imply virginity but doesn't have to mean that. Because of this, many see the likelihood of a dual fulfillment here and suggest that when Isaiah gave this prophecy, a young woman likely became pregnant and bore a son. This birth, some believe, served as a sign to King Ahaz. Later, when Mary became pregnant supernaturally, the prophecy was ultimately fulfilled in the birth of Jesus.

Indeed, two of the Gospel writers used the Greek word parthenos, *which unambiguously means "virgin," to describe Mary's pregnancy with Jesus. "'The virgin will conceive and give birth to a son, and they will call him Immanuel' (which means 'God with us')" (Matthew 1:23; Luke 1:27–35).*

THE HOUSE OF BREAD

Some seven centuries before Jesus was born, the prophet Micah identified Bethlehem, a town just south of Jerusalem, as the birthplace of the Messiah. The name *Bethlehem* is derived from two Hebrew words: *bayit,* which means "house," and *lechem,* which means "bread." Thus, *Bethlehem* literally means "house of bread." Christians find it interesting that the One who later described Himself as the "bread of life" (John 6:35) was born in the "house of bread."

The Messiah's birth would take place in Bethlehem. The prophet Micah predicted the birthplace of Jesus: "But you, Bethlehem Ephrathah, though you are small among the clans of Judah, out of you will come for me one who will be ruler over Israel, whose origins are from of old, from ancient times" (Micah 5:2).

In Matthew 2:1, we read: "After Jesus was born in Bethlehem in Judea, during the time of King Herod, Magi from the east came to Jerusalem."

The Messiah's birth would result in the massacre of innocent children. Jeremiah spoke ominously of grim events surrounding the birth of the Messiah: "This is what the LORD says: 'A voice is heard in Ramah, mourning and great weeping, Rachel weeping for her

"The Massacre of the Innocents" has been depicted in many works of art over the centuries. This one is from the Flemish master Peter Paul Rubens (1577–1640).

children and refusing to be comforted, because they are no more'" (Jeremiah 31:15).

Matthew recorded, "When Herod realized that he had been outwitted by the Magi, he was furious, and he gave orders to kill all the boys in Bethlehem and its vicinity who were two years old and under, in accordance with the time he had learned from the Magi" (Matthew 2:16). Matthew 2:17–18 says this ghastly incident was the fulfillment of Jeremiah's prophecy.

These are only some of the prophecies pertaining to the birth of Jesus. But even these few show the startling accuracy of the ancient prophets. What about Old Testament predictions regarding the life and ministry of Christ? How well did Jesus fulfill those prophecies?

PROPHECIES ABOUT THE MESSIAH'S LIFE AND MINISTRY

The Messiah would be preceded by a messenger. The last of the writing prophets recorded this declaration: "'I will send my messenger, who will prepare the way before me. Then suddenly the Lord you are seeking will come to his temple; the messenger of the covenant, whom you desire, will come,' says the Lᴏʀᴅ Almighty" (Malachi 3:1).

Matthew recorded Jesus talking with His disciples about John the Baptist and claiming, "This is the one about whom it is written: 'I will send my messenger ahead of you, who will prepare your way before you'" (Matthew 11:10; see also Mark 1:2–4, 7).

The Messiah would preach liberty for the captives. Isaiah gave this joyous messianic pronouncement: "The Spirit of the Sovereign Lord is on me, because the Lord has anointed me to proclaim good news to the poor. He has sent me to bind up the broken-hearted, to proclaim freedom for the captives and release from darkness for the prisoners, to proclaim the year of the Lord's favor and the day of vengeance of our God, to comfort all who mourn" (Isaiah 61:1–2).

When Jesus preached in His hometown of Nazareth, He read this passage (see Luke 4:18–19) and declared to the listening crowd, "Today this scripture is fulfilled in your hearing" (Luke 4:21).

The Messiah would minister in Zebulun, Naphtali, and Galilee. Isaiah spoke of blessing coming one day to northern Israel: "Nevertheless, there will be no more gloom for those who were in distress. In the past he humbled the land of Zebulun and the land of Naphtali, but in the future he will honor Galilee of the nations, by the Way of the Sea, beyond the Jordan— The people walking in darkness have seen a great light; on those living in the land of deep darkness a light has dawned" (Isaiah 9:1–2).

Matthew, the writer of the first Gospel, wrote that by beginning His ministry in Galilee—and making that region His base of operations—Jesus fulfilled this ancient prophecy (Matthew 4:12–16).

John the Baptist's father, Zechariah, prophesied upon the birth of his son, "You, my child, will be called a prophet of the Most High; for you will go on before the Lord to prepare the way for him" (Luke 1:76).

WHO IS MELCHIZEDEK?

Psalm 110 contains a strange but fascinating passage. In English, it reads awkwardly at best, but in Hebrew, Yahweh ("the LORD") tells Adonai (the one David called "my lord"—and the one we think of as the Messiah) to sit at His right hand. In the ancient world, to sit at one's right hand meant to occupy a place of influence and authority. David quoted a promise from Yahweh to the Messiah in verse 1: "I [will] make your enemies a footstool for your feet." (It's worth noting that Jesus quoted this passage in reference to Himself in Luke 20:43). A few verses later, still speaking to David's "lord," God said, "You are a priest forever, in the order of Melchizedek" (verse 4). This pronouncement about Melchizedek is so significant that it was quoted in the New Testament book of Hebrews twice (Hebrews 5:6 and 7:17). But what exactly does it mean?

The name *Melchizedek* means "king of righteousness." In the story of Abraham, an enigmatic character named Melchizedek suddenly appeared in Genesis 14, almost out of nowhere. The Bible doesn't give us any background information about Melchizedek. He's simply described as king of Salem and priest of God Most High. The two men shared a meal together. Melchizedek gave bread and wine to Abraham. Abraham honored Melchizedek by giving him a tithe—literally, a tenth—of the spoils he'd just won in battle.

Psalm 110 is a prophecy that Jesus would be a priest like Melchizedek, a priest not by virtue of genealogy but simply due to the call of God (Hebrews 5:6–11; 6:20–7:28). The Levites were the tribe that provided Israel with priests, but Jesus came from the tribe of Judah.

Some maintain that the Melchizedek of Genesis 14 was the preincarnate Jesus come to dine with Abraham. Others see Melchizedek as a type of Christ—that is, a foreshadowing of the perfect king-priest still to come. What is beyond dispute from Psalm 110 is that Jesus lives forever. We can trust that He will continue His work as both King and High Priest into eternity. As the writer of Hebrews declared, "He is able to save completely those who come to God through him" (Hebrews 7:25).

The Messiah would speak in parables. Asaph began one of his psalms with these words: "I will open my mouth with a parable; I will utter hidden things, things from of old" (Psalm 78:2).

When asked by His followers about a parable He'd just told, Jesus replied, "The knowledge of the secrets of the kingdom of God has been given to you, but to others I speak in parables, so that, 'though seeing, they may not see; though hearing, they may not understand'" (Luke 8:10). Some see this statement by Jesus as the ultimate fulfillment of Asaph's words.

Jesus' story of the prodigal son was a parable—what some have described as an earthly story with a heavenly meaning.

The Messiah would be a prophet like Moses. In Deuteronomy, God told Moses of a coming prophet, saying: "I will raise up for them a prophet like you from among their fellow Israelites, and I will put my words in his mouth. He will tell them everything I command him. I myself will call to account anyone who does not listen to my words that the prophet speaks in my name" (Deuteronomy 18:18–19).

When Jesus fed the five thousand, the crowds began saying of Him, "Surely this is the Prophet who is to come into the world" (John 6:14).

The Messiah would care for the poor and needy. In one of the messianic psalms, we read: "For he will deliver the needy who cry out, the afflicted who have no one to help. He will take pity on the weak and the needy and save the needy from death" (Psalm 72:12–13).

When John the Baptist had a personal battle with doubt after he was imprisoned by King Herod, he sent messengers to Jesus to ask Him if He really was the Messiah. Jesus replied, "Go back and report to John what you have seen and heard: The blind receive sight, the lame walk, those who have leprosy are cleansed, the deaf hear, the dead are raised, and the good news is proclaimed to the poor" (Luke 7:22).

The Messiah would have a zeal for God's house, the temple. In Psalm 69, David wrote, "Zeal for your house consumes me" (verse 9).

When Jesus drove the money changers out of the temple, "his disciples remembered that it is written: 'Zeal for your house will consume me'" (John 2:17). They saw David's words as applying ultimately to Jesus.

The Messiah would be a shepherd to His people. Ezekiel prophesied, "I will place over them one shepherd, my servant David, and he will tend them; he will tend them and be their shepherd. I the LORD will be their God, and my servant David will be prince among them. I the LORD have spoken" (Ezekiel 34:23–24).

Because Ezekiel prophesied after David's death, many see in this prophecy a reference to the Son of David (the Messiah), and they note Jesus' claim: "I am the good shepherd. The good shepherd lays down his life for the sheep" (John 10:11).

THE MESSIANIC COLT

Four hundred years before Jesus entered Jerusalem on Palm Sunday riding a donkey, the prophet Zechariah had already described this event: "Rejoice, O people of Zion! Shout in triumph, O people of Jerusalem! Look, your king is coming to you. He is righteous and victorious, yet he is humble, riding on a donkey—riding on a donkey's colt" (Zechariah 9:9 NLT).

Matthew 21:2–5 explains that Jesus told His disciples to fetch this young colt, perhaps so that onlookers would recognize Him as the king that Zechariah had foretold. Both Matthew and the apostle John cited this event as a fulfillment of Zechariah's prophecy (see John 12:15).

Soldiers and kings typically rode into battle on mighty warhorses, but here was a "lowly" king, peacefully riding into the city with gentleness and humility.

Jesus "made a whip out of cords, and drove all from the temple courts, both sheep and cattle; he scattered the coins of the money changers and overturned their tables" (John 2:15).

The Messiah would be rejected by His brothers. David lamented in Psalm 69: "I have become estranged from my brothers and an alien to my mother's sons" (Psalm 69:8 NASB).

In his Gospel, the apostle John noted of Jesus, "For even his own brothers did not believe in him" (John 7:5). Many claim this is a classic example of a prophecy with dual fulfillment—descriptive of David's life and the Messiah's.

While cornerstones are largely ceremonial today, in earlier times they provided direction for the entire building to follow.

The Messiah would be rejected as Israel's cornerstone. In a famous psalm celebrating God's loyal love to Israel, and for giving them victory over their enemies, we find this cryptic statement: "The stone the builders rejected has become the cornerstone; the LORD has done this, and it is marvelous in our eyes" (Psalm 118:22–23).

Matthew recorded Jesus telling a story about a landowner who leased his vineyard to some farmers. When the owner sent his servants to collect a share of the harvest, the tenants mistreated them. When he sent his son, the wicked tenants killed him! After telling this shocking story, Jesus quoted these verses from Psalm 118 and said to the hostile Jewish religious leaders who were resisting His ministry, "Have you never read in the Scriptures: 'The stone the builders rejected has become the cornerstone; the Lord has done this, and it is marvelous in our eyes'?" (Matthew 21:42). Surely Jesus was claiming to be the rejected cornerstone mentioned centuries earlier in the psalm.

Given the many Old Testament prophecies about the *life* of the Messiah, it's not surprising to see numerous ancient predictions surrounding His *death* also.

THE MESSIANIC BEAUTY OF PSALM 118

The Jewish people have always regarded Psalm 118 as a messianic psalm. In ancient times they would sing its stirring lyrics as they traveled up to Jerusalem for their annual festivals. "LORD, save us! LORD, grant us success! Blessed is he who comes in the name of the LORD. From the house of the LORD we bless you" (verses 25–26).

Over the centuries, the Festival of Tabernacles took on a strong messianic dimension. The pilgrims streaming into Jerusalem would pray for the coming Messiah and yearn for the day when God would dwell with His people once more. At the end of this eight-day celebration, Israel's high priest would lead a procession to the pool of Siloam for what was called the "water celebration." At the pool, he would fill a gold pitcher with water, return to the temple, and pour it out. During this glad procession, the priests would continuously recite Psalm 118—and other pilgrim songs, too.

In John 7, we read that Jesus, near the end of His earthly ministry, attended the Festival of Tabernacles in Jerusalem. On the last and greatest day of that festival—possibly as the water ceremony was taking place—Jesus stood and cried out in a loud voice: "Let anyone who is thirsty come to me and drink. Whoever believes in me, as Scripture has said, rivers of living water will flow from within them" (verses 37–38).

Remarkable! This was Jesus' way of saying, "This psalm, this festival, and this ritual are all about Me."

PROPHECIES ABOUT THE MESSIAH'S DEATH

The Messiah's enemies would plot to kill God's anointed. In Psalm 31, David expressed great need in the face of persecution. Most see this as a messianic psalm. In verse 13, David wrote, "For I hear many whispering, 'Terror on every side!' They conspire against me and plot to take my life."

Some see veiled in this verse at least an allusion, if not an outright prophecy, to the conspiracy against Jesus, the Son of David. Speaking of Jesus' enemies, Matthew wrote: "Early in the morning, all the chief priests and the elders of the people made their plans how to have Jesus executed" (Matthew 27:1).

The Messiah would be betrayed. Many see a clear messianic prophecy in Psalm 41, where David wrote, "Even my close friend, someone I trusted, one who shared my bread, has turned against me" (verse 9). He was likely referring to Ahithophel, one of his cabinet members (see 2 Samuel 15:12); however, this verse also seems to hint at Judas's betrayal of Jesus.

In Mark 14, Jesus said, "'Truly I tell you, one of you will betray me— one who is eating with me.' They were saddened, and one by one they said to him, 'Surely you don't mean me?'

'It is one of the Twelve,' he replied, 'one who dips bread into the bowl with me'" (verses 18–20).

Judas Iscariot, one of the twelve disciples, agrees to betray Jesus to the Jewish religious leaders for thirty pieces of silver.

A SAVIOR FOR THE WHOLE WORLD

The prophet Isaiah wrote of a glorious coming day in which "the heir to David's throne will be a banner of salvation to all the world" (Isaiah 11:10 NLT).

This verse uses the Hebrew word *goyim* to speak of non-Jewish people. *Goyim* was the word often used to denote "pagan foreigners." But here the prophet foretold of a Jewish savior who will save "others, too, besides [God's] people Israel" (Isaiah 56:8 NLT). What a fantastic promise: Jews and Gentiles alike can be rescued from sin and brought into right standing with God.

Actually, we should not be surprised. Long before God revealed this to Isaiah, He had already promised Abraham, "All peoples on earth will be blessed through you" (Genesis 12:3). And Jesus' final words to His disciples were a command to "go and make disciples of all nations" (Matthew 28:19).

Questioned by a servant girl in the high priest's courtyard, Peter denies he even knows Jesus.

The Messiah would be abandoned by all. In Psalm 31, David groaned, "Because of all my enemies, I am the utter contempt of my neighbors and an object of dread to my closest friends—those who see me on the street flee from me" (verse 11).

The Gospels tell us that when Jesus was arrested, "everyone deserted him and fled" (Mark 14:50).

The Messiah would be quiet before His accusers. In Psalm 38, David was lamenting his dire situation. He wrote, "Those who want to kill me set their traps, those who would harm me talk of my ruin; all day long they scheme and lie. I am like the deaf, who cannot hear, like the mute, who cannot speak" (verses 12–13)

Some see this as a prophecy, or at least a foreshadowing, of how Jesus would later be silent and give no answer in the face of multiple accusations.

Matthew wrote: "Then Pilate asked him, 'Don't you hear the testimony they are bringing against you?' But Jesus made no reply, not even to a single charge—to the great amazement of the governor" (27:13-14).

The Messiah would be beaten and spat upon. In one of his famous "Servant of the LORD" passages, the prophet Isaiah declared (of the Messiah), "I offered my back to those who beat me, my cheeks to those who pulled out my beard; I did not hide my face from mocking and spitting" (Isaiah 50:6).

In a powerful sermon after Pentecost, Peter accused the people of Jerusalem of killing Jesus: "This man was handed over to you by God's deliberate plan and foreknowledge; and you, with the help of wicked men, put him to death by nailing him to the cross" (Acts 2:23).

JESUS PROPHESIED HIS OWN DEATH

At multiple times during the latter stages of His earthly ministry, Jesus Himself foretold His stunned disciples about His impending suffering and death:

✳ "From that time on Jesus began to explain to his disciples that he must go to Jerusalem and suffer many things at the hands of the elders, the chief priests and the teachers of the law, and that he must be killed and on the third day be raised to life" (Matthew 16:21).

✳ "He then began to teach them that the Son of Man must suffer many things and be rejected by the elders, the chief priests and the teachers of the law, and that he must be killed and after three days rise again" (Mark 8:31).

✳ "And he said, 'The Son of Man must suffer many things and be rejected by the elders, the chief priests and the teachers of the law, and he must be killed and on the third day be raised to life'" (Luke 9:22).

Matthew's Gospel describes Jesus being flogged (27:26). Matthew added, "Then they knelt in front of him and mocked him. 'Hail, king of the Jews!' they said. They spit on him, and took the staff and struck him on the head again and again" (27:29-30).

The Messiah's executioners would pierce His hands and feet. Psalm 22, ascribed to David, reads almost like a reporter's eyewitness description of Jesus' crucifixion. David wrote, "A pack of villains encircles me; they pierce my hands and my feet" (verse 16).

Likewise, the apostle John, after describing the crucifixion from beginning to bitter end, wrote, "These things happened so that the scripture would be fulfilled: 'Not one of his bones will be broken,' and, as another scripture says, 'They will look on the one they have pierced'" (John 19:36-37).

The Messiah's enemies would cast lots for His clothing. In Psalm 22, we find another breathtaking prediction. In David's words, "They divide my clothes among them and cast lots for my garment" (verse 18).

In John's account of the crucifixion, we read, "When the soldiers crucified Jesus, they took his clothes, dividing them into four shares, one for each
of them, with the undergarment remaining. This garment was seamless,
woven in one piece from top to bottom. 'Let's not tear it,' they said to one
another. 'Let's decide by lot who will get it.' This happened that the scripture might be fulfilled that said, 'They divided my clothes among them and
cast lots for my garment.' So this is what the soldiers did" (John 19:23–24).

The Messiah would be forsaken. In David's Psalm 22 lament, he
cried, "My God, my God, why have you forsaken me? Why are you so
far from saving me, so far from my cries of anguish?" (verse 1).

In Matthew's account of Jesus' execution, he wrote, "About three in the
afternoon Jesus cried out in a loud voice, 'Eli, Eli, lema sabachthani?' (which
means 'My God, my God, why have you forsaken me?')" (Matthew 27:46).

Within the vast catalog of crucifixion art, nothing can adequately convey Jesus' anguish
as He cried out to His Father, "Why have you forsaken me?" (Matthew 27:46).

The Messiah would be mocked and scorned. In Psalm 22, David mentioned the disdainful comments of his enemies: "'He trusts in the LORD,' they say, 'let the LORD rescue him. Let him deliver him, since he delights in him'" (verse 8).

Jesus' enemies engaged in this same sort of derisive catcalling as He hung on the cross: "'He saved others,' they said, 'but he can't save himself! He's the king of Israel! Let him come down now from the cross, and we will believe in him. He trusts in God. Let God rescue him now if he wants him, for he said, "I am the Son of God"'" (Matthew 27:42–43).

The Messiah would be thirsty. In Psalm 22, David mentioned his agonizing thirst, "My mouth is dried up like a potsherd, and my tongue sticks to the roof of my mouth; you lay me in the dust of death" (verse 15).

John obviously saw this as a prophecy with dual fulfillment, because he wrote, "Later, knowing that everything had now been finished, and so that Scripture would be fulfilled, Jesus said, 'I am thirsty'" (John 19:28).

The Messiah would commit His spirit into God's hands. David said in Psalm 31, "Into your hands I commit my spirit" (verse 5).

Luke wrote, "Jesus called out with a loud voice, 'Father, into your hands I commit my spirit'" (Luke 23:46).

The Messiah's betrayer would be replaced. In Psalm 109, David wrote of one of his enemies, "May another take his place of leadership" (verse 8).

After Judas Iscariot hung himself, Peter referenced Psalm 109, saying, "It is written in the Book of Psalms: 'May his place be deserted; let there be no one to dwell in it,' and, 'May another take his place of leadership'" (Acts 1:20). Sure enough, after casting lots, the apostles appointed Matthias to take the place of Judas (Acts 1:26).

The remarkably accurate prophecies don't stop with Jesus' death. They also foretell His resurrection.

PROPHECIES ABOUT THE MESSIAH'S RESURRECTION AND ASCENSION

The Messiah would not see decay. In Psalm 16, we read these prophetic words of David: "Therefore my heart is glad and my tongue rejoices; my body also will rest secure, because you will not abandon me to the realm of the dead, nor will you let your faithful one see decay" (verses 9–10).

The apostle Peter quoted this verse during his Pentecost sermon, saying, "Seeing what was to come, he spoke of the resurrection of the Messiah, that he was not abandoned to the realm of the dead, nor did his body see decay" (Acts 2:31).

Mary Magdalene reaches for the resurrected Jesus as an angel observes from the empty tomb. Jesus was in the grave for parts of three days.

The Messiah would ascend to glory. Psalm 68 is a song of victory written by King David after he defeated one of his enemies, set free some prisoners, and gained the spoils of war. The specific victory described is unclear, but it is possibly the conquering of the Jebusite fortress—that is, the ancient city of Jerusalem (see 2 Samuel 5:7)—or perhaps the return of the ark of the covenant to Jerusalem (2 Samuel 6:12–15). The occasion of the victory doesn't matter so much as what it signified: the rule of God in His holy city.

Psalm 68:18 says, "When you ascended on high, you took many captives; you received gifts from people, even from the rebellious—that you, Lᴏʀᴅ God, might dwell there."

Forty days after the resurrection, Jesus was talking with His disciples when "he was taken up before their very eyes, and a cloud hid him from their sight" (Acts 1:9).

DID JESUS *REALLY* CLAIM TO BE THE MESSIAH?

Some critics have alleged that Jesus never claimed to be the long-awaited Messiah, that this was a title His followers ascribed to Him. According to the Gospels, however, Jesus said He was the Messiah predicted in the Old Testament.

❋ *While talking to a Samaritan woman at Jacob's well:* "The woman said, 'I know that Messiah' (called Christ) 'is coming. When he comes, he will explain everything to us.' Then Jesus declared, 'I, the one speaking to you—I am he'" (John 4:25–26).

❋ *While talking with His disciples:* "'But what about you?' he asked. 'Who do you say I am?' Simon Peter answered, 'You are the Messiah, the Son of the living God.' Jesus replied, 'Blessed are you, Simon son of Jonah, for this was not revealed to you by flesh and blood, but by my Father in heaven'" (Matthew 16:15–17; see also Mark 8:29–30; Luke 9:20–21).

❋ *While standing trial before the Jewish leaders:* "But Jesus remained silent and gave no answer. Again the high priest asked him, 'Are you the Messiah, the Son of the Blessed One?' 'I am,' said Jesus. 'And you will see the Son of Man sitting at the right hand of the Mighty One and coming on the clouds of heaven'" (Mark 14:61–62; see also Matthew 26:63–66, which tells of the high priest tearing his clothes and charging Jesus with blasphemy).

When we consider Jesus' statements, we would be wise to embrace the airtight logic of C. S. Lewis. If Jesus' claims are false, they are of no importance. But if they are true, they are of infinite importance. The one thing they cannot be? Semi-important.

"You have heard the blasphemy," the high priest shouts, after Jesus answers "I am" to the question, "Are you the Messiah, the Son of the Blessed One?" (Mark 14:61–64).

In the New Testament, the apostle Paul quoted this passage in Ephesians 4:8 and applied it to Jesus, who, through His death on the cross, set free those who were held captive by sin. After ascending to heaven, he distributed gifts of the Spirit to His followers. Those who believe Jesus will one day rule the earth from a literal throne in Jerusalem claim that Psalm 68:28–35 hints at the fact that during that time, kings from all over the world will bring gifts to the Messiah because the whole world will worship Him.

We started this chapter with a fascinating story from Luke 24: the resurrected Jesus talking with and teaching two of His unsuspecting followers on the road to Emmaus.

Luke wrote that as they got close to their destination, "Jesus continued on as if he were going farther. But they urged him strongly, 'Stay with us, for it is nearly evening; the day is almost over.' So he went in to stay with them. When he was at the table with them, he took bread, gave thanks, broke it and began to give it to them. Then their eyes were opened and they recognized him, and he disappeared from their sight. They asked each other, 'Were not our hearts burning within us while he talked with us on the road and opened the Scriptures to us?'" (Luke 24:28–32).

The two men immediately returned to Jerusalem to report their experience to the apostles. As they were talking, Jesus suddenly stood among the larger group. After a time of understandable shock and excitement, Jesus "said to them, 'This is what I told you while I was still with you: Everything must be fulfilled that is written about me in the Law of Moses, the Prophets and the Psalms.' Then he opened their minds so they could understand the Scriptures" (Luke 24:44–45).

According to Jesus, the entire Old Testament points to Him. Centuries before the coming of Jesus, God tipped His hand. He gave the world a sneak preview of all He had planned.

What are the implications of these messianic prophecies being fulfilled in the life of Jesus? At least two: (1) The Bible is not just any book, and (2) Jesus is not just an inspiring teacher.

Part Two:

PROPHECIES PENDING

Chapter 7:
PROPHECIES BY JESUS

In the previous chapter, we looked briefly at some of the numerous Old Testaments prophecies regarding the Messiah. We saw how those ancient predictions were fulfilled to the smallest detail in the birth, life, ministry, death, and resurrection of Jesus.

There's no getting around it: Jesus is *the* great focus of biblical prophecy. The prophets and kings of the Old Testament looked forward to His coming. The New Testament apostles marveled at His coming and eagerly anticipated His future second coming.

But Jesus—as Messiah—also fulfilled the role of prophet. In fact, He was the great prophet of whom Moses spoke when the people of Israel were poised to enter the Promised Land (see Deuteronomy 18:15–18).

PROPHECY IN THE NEW TESTAMENT

We've said that a prophet is one who is called by God to speak for God. Simply put, a prophet's speech involves either *forthtelling* (announcing the truth of God in a forthright way) or *foretelling* (revealing God's plans in advance). Typically, when we think of prophets, we think of the legendary Old Testament prophets—spiritual giants like Isaiah and Jeremiah, Daniel and Elijah. Because of their stature, it's easy to forget that the prophetic tradition continued into the New Testament era, with figures such as John the Baptist and Anna (Luke 2:36).

Many in first-century Israel recognized Jesus as a prophet. Matthew recorded that the people watching Jesus ride into Jerusalem on a donkey on Palm Sunday exclaimed, "This is Jesus, the prophet from Nazareth in Galilee" (Matthew 21:11). John wrote about an encounter Jesus had with a Samaritan woman at Jacob's well. When the Lord rattled off this woman's relational history with men within minutes of meeting her, she replied, "Sir, I can see that you are a prophet" (John 4:19).

Jesus admitted the prophetic nature of His teaching when He said, "My teaching is not my own. It comes from the one who sent me" (John 7:16). Another time Jesus declared, "For I did not speak on my own, but the Father who sent me commanded me to say all that I have spoken" (John 12:49).

Jesus was so much more than a prophet, but He was a prophet. Many say His most important prophecy was His Olivet Discourse (see Matthew 24–25, Mark 13, and Luke 21:37–38). All other prophecies—Old Testament and New—point ahead to the events Jesus described here: the end of the age, the second coming of Christ, and the new world to come.

Since every prophecy regarding the first coming of the Messiah has been fulfilled, we can have confidence that every one of Jesus' prophetic words will come to pass as well.

"This is Jesus, the prophet from Nazareth in Galilee," people said during Jesus' triumphal entry into Jerusalem (Matthew 21:11).

In this chapter we want to look not at prophecies *about* Jesus but at prophecies *by* Him. We'll mention some of the prophecies He made that were fulfilled in His lifetime or shortly after. Mostly, we'll focus on the prophecies of Jesus that are still awaiting fulfillment.

JESUS' PROPHECIES ABOUT THE CHURCH

Matthew recorded a discussion in which Jesus probed to see whether His followers understood His true identity. When Peter blurted out, "You are the Messiah, the Son of the living God," Jesus responded by saying, "Blessed are you, Simon son of Jonah, for this was not revealed to you by flesh and blood, but by my Father in heaven. And I tell you that you are Peter, and on this rock I will build my church, and the gates of Hades will not overcome it" (Matthew 16:16–18).

Don't miss the enormous prophecy found in verse 18. Jesus declared, "I will build my church." What is the church? The Greek word translated *church* is *ekklesia*, and it means "assembly" or "congregation." The New Testament describes the church as all the people who put their trust in Jesus. The word can refer to all believers worldwide, or it can refer to all the believers in a particular locale.

Most Christians agree that Jesus inaugurated the global spread of the church when He poured out the Holy Spirit on His followers who were gathered in Jerusalem in about AD 30

This Christian church building houses a congregation in the southeast Asian island nation of Indonesia.

GREJA KRISTEN JAWI WETAN
JEMAAT MOJOWARNO
(BADAN HUKUM № 53/TGL 27-8-1932/STBL № 372)

for the Jewish festival of Pentecost (Acts 2). Jesus was the cornerstone of this new work of God, and the apostles and prophets were the foundation (Ephesians 2:20). If we accept this idea, then it's fair to say that Jesus has been busy building His church—and fulfilling this prophecy—for some two thousand years. People around the world continue to hear the Gospel and believe in Jesus daily, thereby joining Christ's church. Jesus' great building project is not finished yet.

JESUS' PROPHECIES ABOUT JERUSALEM

Throughout the Gospels, Jesus is shown expressing His undying love—and righteous frustration—with the not-always-holy city of Jerusalem.

In Luke 13, His tone is sorrowful: "Jerusalem, Jerusalem, you who kill the prophets and stone those sent to you, how often I have longed

This 1867 painting by Francesco Hayez portrays the destruction of the Jerusalem temple in AD 70, an event Jesus seemed to predict several decades earlier.

to gather your children together, as a hen gathers her chicks under her wings, and you were not willing. Look, your house is left to you desolate. I tell you, you will not see me again until you say, 'Blessed is he who comes in the name of the Lord'" (verses 34–35). Jesus quoted Psalm 118:26 here, and many take His words as a kind of curse. Their meaning? Jesus seems to be saying, "Because you as a nation are rejecting Me as your promised Messiah, you will not have the chance to welcome Me until I come again."

Later in Luke, His words about Israel's capital city were more ominous. "For the days will come upon you when your enemies will throw up a barricade against you, and surround you and hem you in on every side, and they will level you to the ground and your children within you, and they will not leave in you one stone upon another, because you did not recognize the time of your visitation" (19:43–44 NASB).

Most experts agree that this is a reference to the Roman destruction of Jerusalem in AD 70. Luke recorded similar comments by Jesus a couple of chapters later: "Some of his disciples were remarking about how the temple was adorned with beautiful stones and with gifts dedicated to God. But Jesus said, 'As for what you see here, the time will come when not one stone will be left on another; every one of them will be thrown down'" (21:5–6).

JESUS' PROPHECIES ABOUT FRUITFUL LIVING

The Beatitudes. In His famous Sermon on the Mount, Jesus talked about the ethical character that would mark His kingdom and its subjects. Some scholars say believers should apply these teachings in a spiritual way to life right now. Others insist these words of Jesus are the governing principles of a literal future kingdom that will be established when Christ returns. Some see truth in both views and say that believers should live out these principles now and rest in Jesus' promise that one day the whole world will live by them.

The sermon begins with a series of cryptic sayings known as the Beatitudes (Matthew 5:1–12). These beloved maxims predict divine favor for saints facing various situations, some of them dire. Jesus prophesied assorted blessings. The word *blessed* literally suggests true spiritual happiness. His blessings are for people who are spiritually poor, who mourn, who are humble, who yearn to be right with God, who are merciful and pure in heart, who pursue peace with others, and who suffer persecution for living in the way of Christ.

Most Christians can attest to having experienced this kind of "holy happiness" at times in life. All devoted followers of Jesus want to become "beatitude believers." They trust Jesus daily for joy now and for ultimate blessing when His kingdom comes in full.

This statue, near the Sea of Galilee, commemorates Jesus' teaching known as the Beatitudes recorded in Matthew 5.

The Vine and the Branches.
John 13–17 records Jesus'
final instructions to His closest followers on the night
before His crucifixion. During
this extended teaching time,
Jesus explained how their
lives might be a blessing to
the world: "Remain in me, as I
also remain in you. No branch
can bear fruit by itself; it must
remain in the vine. Neither
can you bear fruit unless you
remain in me. I am the vine;
you are the branches. If you
remain in me and I in you, you
will bear much fruit; apart
from me you can do nothing"
(John 15:4–5).

Grapes grow from the branches, which draw
nourishment from the vine—a picture of the
spiritual life that Jesus taught in John 15.

Using the agricultural imagery of a healthy grapevine with lots
of branches loaded with grapes, Jesus told His followers they
could expect this outcome: *If you will stay connected to Me,
My life and power will flow through your life and
bring blessing to others.* This is a spiritual
reality that has been fulfilled in the lives of
believers throughout history. And it is a
prophecy/promise that continues to be
realized.

PROPHECIES BY JESUS, FULFILLED DURING THE LIFE OF JESUS (OR SOON AFTER HIS RESURRECTION)

Throughout Jesus' ministry, we see Him announcing or predicting things. Many of these prophecies came to pass in short order. Here are just a few examples from the Gospels:

✳ Jesus told His first disciples He would turn them into evangelists: "Follow Me . . . and I will make you fishers of men" (Matthew 4:19 NASB). This happened in Matthew 10:1–6 and Matthew 28:18–20.

✳ Jesus told a royal official who had come from Capernaum to ask Jesus to heal his desperately ill son, "Go . . . your son will live" (John 4:50). The man arrived home to find the boy completely recovered.

✳ Jesus prophesied the resurrection of Lazarus; then He called His friend out of the grave (John 11).

✳ Jesus told a couple of His followers where to find a donkey He could ride into Jerusalem on Palm Sunday (Mark 11:1–6). The men found the donkey exactly where Jesus said it would be.

✳ When Jesus gave Peter and John instructions about where to set up the Passover celebration known as the Last Supper, He told them to look for a man carrying a jar of water who would lead them to the proper place. All this happened just as Jesus said (Luke 22:7–13).

✳ Jesus predicted that Judas would betray Him (Matthew 26:20–25). This is exactly what transpired (see Matthew 26:47–50).

✳ Jesus foretold that His disciples would desert Him. "This very night you will all fall away on account of me" (Matthew 26:31). Matthew was one of those disciples. He reported that only a short time later "all the disciples deserted him and fled" (Matthew 26:56).

✳ Jesus prophesied Peter's denial: "Truly I tell you . . . this very night, before the rooster crows, you will disown me three times" (Matthew 26:34). It happened just as Jesus predicted.

✳ Jesus foretold His coming condemnation, humiliation, death, and resurrection (Mark 10:32–34). Every part of His prophetic announcement came true (see Mark 15–16).

After four days in the tomb, Lazarus returns to life—just as Jesus had predicted.

JESUS' PROPHECIES ABOUT THE BLESSING OF FOLLOWING HIM

Jesus had a conversation with a wealthy young man. He urged the man to give his great fortune to the poor so that he might have treasure in heaven. "Then come, follow me" (Mark 10:21), Jesus insisted. Mark wrote, "At this the man's face fell. He went away sad, because he had great wealth" (Mark 10:22).

Jesus used this exchange to warn His followers about the dangers of worldly wealth to one's spiritual condition. Peter then reminded Jesus that he and the other disciples *had* left everything to follow Him. "'Truly I tell you,' Jesus replied, 'no one who has left home or brothers or sisters or mother or father or children or fields for me

A wealthy young man asks Jesus how to gain eternal life—but can't accept Jesus' answer.

and the gospel will fail to receive a hundred times as much in this present age: homes, brothers, sisters, mothers, children and fields—along with persecutions—and in the age to come eternal life. But many who are first will be last, and the last first'" (Mark 10:28–31).

This promise/prophecy from Jesus has been fulfilled countless times in the lives of God's faithful servants through the centuries—and it is still being experienced. Here are some examples.

Carl, a Christian attorney, turned his back on a lucrative career in corporate law to become a public defender. As a result of this decision, Carl doesn't make nearly what his law school buddies make. But he finds unearthly joy in serving those who can't afford legal representation.

Marie is a teacher at a missionary school in Asia. She doesn't own a car or a home, doesn't have a husband or supportive family or any kind of retirement plan. Yet she has traveled extensively, seen beautiful places, and met wonderful people. She's been loved deeply by generous surrogate families across three continents. Marie would tell you that while it may look like she has very little, her life is acually full of blessing.

David Livingstone was a Scottish doctor and missionary who devoted his life to serving God by serving the African people. In 1857 during an address to students at Cambridge University, he said, "People talk of the sacrifice I have made in spending so much of my life in Africa. . . . Is that a sacrifice which brings its own blest reward in healthful

Subject of the famous question, "Dr. Livingstone, I presume?" David Livingstone (1813–1873) was both an explorer of and missionary to Africa.

activity, the consciousness of doing good, peace of mind, and a bright hope of a glorious destiny hereafter? . . . It is emphatically no sacrifice. Say rather it is a privilege. . . . I never made a sacrifice."

Jesus' promise is still operational: the Lord blesses His faithful servants, both now and forever, in all sorts of unexpected ways. This prophecy is echoed in some of Jesus' parables—for example the parable of the talents, or minas (Luke 19:11–27).

JESUS' PROPHECIES ABOUT THE HOLY SPIRIT

The apostle John recorded several instances in which Jesus prophesied the coming of the Holy Spirit.

The first was when Jesus, on the final day of the Festival of Tabernacles, cried out, "Let anyone who is thirsty come to me and drink. Whoever believes in me, as Scripture has said, rivers of living water will flow from within them" (John 7:37–38). John added that Jesus was referring to the Spirit, "whom those who believed in him were later to receive. Up to that time the Spirit had not been given, since Jesus had not yet been glorified" (John 7:39).

In Jesus' final meeting with His followers—that is, in the upper room the same night of His arrest (see John 13–17)—Jesus prophesied two more times about the coming of the Spirit. First, He said, "When the Advocate comes, whom I will send to you from the Father—the Spirit of truth who goes out from the Father—he will testify about me. And you also must testify, for you have been with me from the beginning" (John 15:26–27).

Then He added:

> "But very truly I tell you, it is for your good that I am going away. Unless I go away, the Advocate will not come to you; but if I go, I will send him to you. When he comes, he will prove the world to be in the wrong about sin and righteousness and judgment:

about sin, because people do not believe in me; about righteousness, because I am going to the Father, where you can see me no longer; and about judgment, because the prince of this world now stands condemned.

"I have much more to say to you, more than you can now bear. But when he, the Spirit of truth, comes, he will guide you into all the truth. He will not speak on his own; he will speak only what he hears, and he will tell you what is yet to come. He will glorify me because it is from me that he will receive what he will make known to you. All that belongs to the Father is mine. That is why I said the Spirit will receive from me what he will make known to you." (John 16:7–15)

There is disagreement among theologians, preachers, and Bible scholars as to how this prophecy has been or will be fulfilled. Some argue that it came to pass when the Holy Spirit descended supernaturally and dramatically on the Jewish believers in Jesus who were gathered for Pentecost in Jerusalem just fifty days after the resurrection (see Acts 2). There is good biblical support for this view; Acts tells us that the Spirit-filled Peter saw what was happening before his eyes and claimed the events were a fulfillment of things predicted long before by the prophet Joel. "I will pour out my Spirit on all people. Your sons and daughters will prophesy, your old men will dream dreams, your young men will see visions. Even on my servants, both men and women, I will pour out my Spirit in those days" (Joel 2:28–29).

Joel, in the next breath, mentioned "the coming of the great and dreadful day of the LORD" (Joel 2:31). Because of this, some people think the ultimate bestowal of the Spirit will be fulfilled in the future, at the second coming of Jesus. As is often the case, some see a dual fulfillment—the gift of the Spirit at Pentecost and a greater outpouring at Christ's return. In the midst of all these interpretations, there is disagreement as to what is meant by "all people." Does that apply to Israel, the church, or all individuals on earth?

Her is what we can say for sure: The Holy Spirit descended at Pentecost and filled the followers of Jesus. This divine enablement gave them supernatural power to be witnesses for Christ, thus fulfilling another prophecy Jesus made about the Spirit just before He ascended into heaven (see Acts 1:8). According to the apostle Paul, this filling of the Spirit is still available to all believers (Ephesians 5:18). In other words, it has happened in the past, is happening in the present, and will continue to happen in the lives of yielded believers until Christ returns.

The sound of a rushing wind and the appearance of tongues of fire above each person accompanied the arrival of the Holy Spirit during the holiday called Pentecost.

JESUS' PROPHECIES ABOUT PERSECUTION

Many of Jesus' prophecies are a source of great comfort for His followers:

* ✳ "Blessed are the pure in heart, for they will see God" (Matthew 5:8).
* ✳ "Whoever acknowledges me before others, I will also acknowledge before my Father in heaven" (Matthew 10:32).
* ✳ "My peace I give you" (John 14:27).

We often turn these promises into memes and social media posts, or we hang them on the wall above the couch. But what about Jesus' less-positive predictions, the ones that cause our hearts to skip a beat, the prophecies about being mistreated because we follow Jesus?

* ✳ "Blessed are you when people insult you, persecute you and falsely say all kinds of evil against you because of me. Rejoice and be glad, because great is your reward in heaven, for in the same way they persecuted the prophets who were before you" (Matthew 5:11–12).
* ✳ "If the world hates you, keep in mind that it hated me first. If you belonged to the world, it would love you as its own. As it is, you do not belong to the world, but I have chosen you out of the world. That is why the world hates you. Remember what I told you: 'A servant is not greater

than his master.' If they persecuted me, they will persecute you also. If they obeyed my teaching, they will obey yours also. They will treat you this way because of my name, for they do not know the one who sent me" (John 15:18–21).

✳ "All this I have told you so that you will not fall away. They will put you out of the synagogue; in fact, the time is coming when anyone who kills you will think they are offering a service to God. They will do such things because they have not known the Father or me. I have told you this, so that when their time comes you will remember that I warned you about them. I did not tell you this from the beginning because I was with you" (John 16:1–4).

The ancient Colosseum of Rome is bathed in red February 24, 2018, during a ceremony honoring persecuted Christians around the world.

These prophecies have been fulfilled throughout history in stomach-turning ways. Truth be told, these grim predictions are being fulfilled around the world even as you read this sentence. There is no guarantee that Christians in any nation will be shielded from trouble—in fact, just the opposite. However, we are promised that Jesus will be with us always (Matthew 28:20).

JESUS' PROPHECIES ABOUT HIS SECOND COMING

The Gospels contain multiple instances of Jesus speaking about returning to the earth in the future:

* ✳ "For the Son of Man is going to come in his Father's glory with his angels, and then he will reward each person according to what they have done" (Matthew 16:27).
* ✳ "Therefore keep watch, because you do not know on what day your Lord will come" (Matthew 24:42).
* ✳ "At that time they will see the Son of Man coming in a cloud with power and great glory" (Luke 21:27).

"If the owner of the house had known at what time of night the thief was coming, he would have kept watch and would not have let his house be broken into," Jesus taught. "So you also must be ready, because the Son of Man will come at an hour when you do not expect him" (Matthew 24:43–44).

PROPHECY IN THE PARABLES

Jesus was a master teacher. He spoke about common, everyday objects and practices to illustrate spiritual realities. He employed simple stories called parables. The Greek word *parabole* means "something placed alongside." Thus a parable was a short, provocative, witty story that compared two things, people, or situations.

Parables typically focused on the coming kingdom of God and who would inhabit it. They contrasted good and evil, the sacred and profane. All this made them perfect for prophetic discourse.

Jesus did not invent parables; the Old Testament prophets used parables, too. Isaiah once conveyed a parable about a vineyard. His purpose? To warn of coming judgment on the people of God for being unfruitful (Isaiah 5:1–7). On another occasion, he used the common practices of plowing and sowing to illustrate God's coming judgment (Isaiah

A fresco of Jesus sowing seed. In a parable, He used this idea to teach about the spreading of the Gospel.

28:23–29). The prophet Habakkuk utilized the image of a fisherman worshiping his nets to describe the godless Babylonians who would soon invade Judah (Habakkuk 1:13–17). Ezekiel employed other creative parables to picture Israel's past, present, and future.

After Jesus told His famous story about a sower indiscriminately casting seeds across a field, His disciples "came to him and asked, 'Why do you speak to the people in parables?' He replied, 'Because the knowledge of the secrets of the kingdom of heaven has been given to you, but not to them'" (Matthew 13:10–11). The book of Hebrews explains Jesus' response: "For we also have had the good news proclaimed to us, just as they did; *but the message they heard was of no value to them, because they did not share the faith of those who obeyed*" (Hebrews 4:2, emphasis added). In short, Jesus used parables because they hid His truth from people who refused to trust Him. But to those who embraced His message, parables offered deeper spiritual understanding.

In addition, Jesus told several parables during His Olivet Discourse: the evil servant and faithful servant in Matthew 24:45–51; the ten virgins in Matthew 25:1–13; the bags of gold (or talents) in Matthew 25:14–30. These stories speak about His return to reign as earth's King.

As we will see in a future chapter, there is much disagreement about the timing of the Lord's return. Some believe He will first come *for* His saints in an event famously called the rapture. They argue that Jesus will appear in the sky and all believers will be "snatched up" to meet the Lord in the air. Proponents of this view cite passages such as 1 Thessalonians 4:13–18 and John 14:1–3 for support. They believe that following a period of terrible tribulation on the earth—either three and a half years or seven years after the rapture occurs—the Lord will return triumphantly *with* His saints in the event commonly called the second coming

JESUS' PROPHECIES ABOUT COMING JUDGMENT

One of the clear and consistent teachings of Jesus during His earthly ministry was that each person will face a day of reckoning. In other words, judgment is coming. As one old preacher put it, "There is a payday someday." Indeed, nobody gets away with *anything*.

The Bible declares that "God is a righteous judge" (Psalm 7:11). Because He is holy, all wrongs *must* be addressed and all sins *must* be punished. The good news of the Christian Gospel, however, is that

The lightning bolt is often used as a lighthearted image for God's wrath. But there is nothing funny about the power of either.

those who trust in Jesus—in His perfect life, sacrificial death, and glorious resurrection—do not have to fear judgment. This is because Jesus willingly took upon Himself the punishment all sinners deserve. In death, He was judged for the sins of the world (1 John 2:2). Therefore, all who trust in Him enjoy full forgiveness, get credit for His righteousness, receive right standing with God, and enjoy new, eternal life. Believers are safe from judgment because they are "in Christ" (Romans 8:1).

On the other hand, those who reject the grace and mercy of God—specifically the payment that Jesus made for their sins and the forgiveness He offers—must stand before God in judgment and answer

Jesus sits in judgment in a sculpture from Paris's famed Cathedral of Notre Dame.

for and pay for their own sins. God will not turn a deaf eye or ear to even the "smallest" evil. If He ignored sin, or winked at injustice, He would cease to be good. He would be an unjust judge (Genesis 18:25).

The Bible further declares that God is a loving Father. Because He is gracious and good, He blesses His people and rewards their faithfulness. The teaching of Jesus and of the entire New Testament is that any acts done out of love for God, and by the power and prompting of the Spirit of God, will be acknowledged and rewarded.

Some read the Bible and see two judgments. The first is a judgment of those who have rejected Christ and spurned the Gospel. This is often referred to as the great white throne judgment (Revelation 20:11–15), a judgment that establishes the guilt and eternal destiny of *unbelievers*. The second is an assessment of the lives of *believers*. It is often called the judgment seat of Christ (2 Corinthians 5:10). It has nothing to do with a believer's destiny. That issue is settled when, at the moment of faith, a believer receives eternal life (John 3:16). The judgment seat of Christ is for the purpose of distributing rewards to believers for faithful service.

Here are a few examples of Jesus' prophecies about coming judgment for the world, for certain groups, and for individuals:

✳ "Not everyone who says to me, 'Lord, Lord,' will enter the kingdom of heaven, but only the one who does the will of my Father who is in heaven. Many will say to me on that day, 'Lord, Lord, did we not prophesy in your name and in your name drive out demons and in your name perform many miracles?' Then I will tell them plainly, 'I never knew you. Away from me, you evildoers!'" (Matthew 7:21–23).

✳ "Whoever acknowledges me before others, I will also acknowledge before my Father in heaven. But whoever disowns me before others, I will disown before my Father in heaven" (Matthew 10:32–33).

✳ "Whoever welcomes a prophet as a prophet will receive a prophet's reward, and whoever welcomes a righteous person as a righteous person will receive a righteous person's reward. And if anyone gives even a cup of cold water to one of these little ones who is my disciple, truly I tell you, that person will certainly not lose their reward" (Matthew 10:41–42).

Jesus prophesied rewards for even very small acts of service—like giving water to a child.

✳ "His master replied, 'Well done, good and faithful servant! You have been faithful with a few things; I will put you in charge of many things. Come and share your master's happiness!'" (Matthew 25:21, from Jesus' parable of the bags of gold).

✳ "When the Son of Man comes in his glory, and all the angels with him, he will sit on his glorious throne. All the nations will be gathered before him, and he will separate the people one from another as a shepherd separates the sheep from the goats. He will put the sheep on his right and the goats on his left" (Matthew 25:31–33).

✳ "For all those who exalt themselves will be humbled, and those who humble themselves will be exalted" (Luke 14:11).

✳ "But when you give a banquet, invite the poor, the crippled, the lame, the blind, and you will be blessed. Although they cannot repay you, you will be repaid at the resurrection of the righteous" (Luke 14:13–14).

We will talk more about the return of Christ and the final judgment in a subsequent chapter. What we can say here is what we've been saying all along: The written Word of God is full of prophetic passages that have already been fulfilled. And Jesus, the living Word of God (John 1:1, 14), also made many prophetic announcements that have come to pass. This leaves us to ponder, "What about all those prophecies that are still pending?"

Christian apologist Justin Martyr wisely noted, "To declare a thing shall come to pass long before it is in being, and to bring it to pass, this or nothing is the work of God."

God is speaking to us through scripture and through Jesus. We should perk up and pay attention. As the voice from heaven told Peter, James, and John when they saw Jesus glorified during His transfiguration, "This is my Son, whom I have chosen; *listen to him*" (Luke 9:35, emphasis added).

Chapter 8:

PROPHECIES ABOUT ISRAEL'S FUTURE

Modern-day Israel is tiny. Barely larger than 8,600 square miles, it's roughly the size of New Jersey. It measures eighty-five miles from east to west—and that's at its widest point. From top to bottom? A mere 270 miles.

How can a country so small dominate the news? Yet it does. Almost every day we hear stories about security concerns in Tel Aviv or Jerusalem, tensions in the Gaza Strip or the West Bank, and saber rattling between Israel and its enemies in the region. At least from a distance, the Holy Land seems like a powder keg.

What does the Bible say about the future of the Jewish people in the land of Abraham?

A QUICK REVIEW OF ISRAEL'S HISTORY

As we've outlined elsewhere in these pages, the God of the Bible graciously revealed Himself to Abram, an elderly resident of ancient Haran. God called him to leave his home. He promised to lead him, bless him, give him a homeland, and turn him and his infertile wife into a great nation (Genesis 12:1–7). The Old Testament documents how God fulfilled all these wild promises, eventually leading the twelve tribes of Israel into Canaan and establishing them there.

WHAT DOES *DIASPORA* MEAN?

Diaspora means "scattering." The Jewish Diaspora refers to the dispersion of the Jewish people out of the land promised to Abraham by God. There have been three dispersions in history. In 722 BC, the Assyrians invaded Israel and scattered the ten northern tribes across the ancient Near East. In 586 BC, the Babylonians, under King Nebuchadnezzar, exiled many of the people of Judah and Jerusalem to Babylon for seventy years. After their release, some returned to Israel; but many chose to stay in Babylon—what is today Iraq. In AD 70, the third and most complete dispersion occurred. Rome sacked Jerusalem, burned it to the ground, and drove the Jews "from one end of the earth to the other" (Deuteronomy 28:64). It is estimated that of the approximate 14.5 million Jews in the world, almost 6.5 million are living in Israel.

Detail from the Arch of Titus in Rome, showing Roman soldiers after the sack of Jerusalem, AD 70.

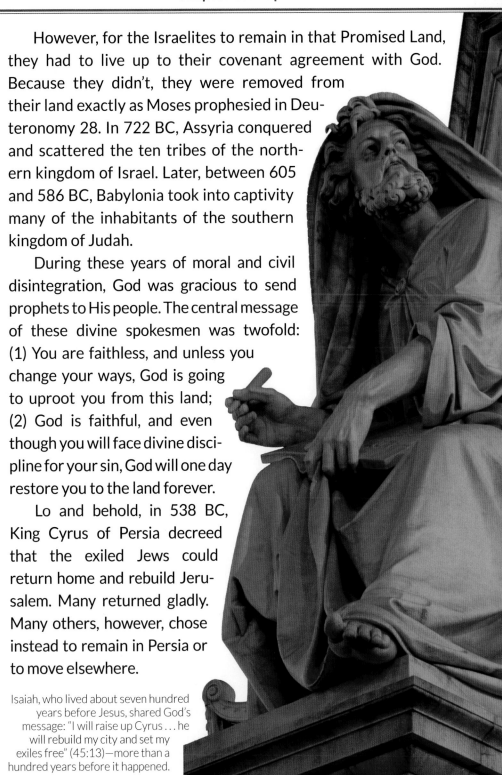

However, for the Israelites to remain in that Promised Land, they had to live up to their covenant agreement with God. Because they didn't, they were removed from their land exactly as Moses prophesied in Deuteronomy 28. In 722 BC, Assyria conquered and scattered the ten tribes of the northern kingdom of Israel. Later, between 605 and 586 BC, Babylonia took into captivity many of the inhabitants of the southern kingdom of Judah.

During these years of moral and civil disintegration, God was gracious to send prophets to His people. The central message of these divine spokesmen was twofold: (1) You are faithless, and unless you change your ways, God is going to uproot you from this land; (2) God is faithful, and even though you will face divine discipline for your sin, God will one day restore you to the land forever.

Lo and behold, in 538 BC, King Cyrus of Persia decreed that the exiled Jews could return home and rebuild Jerusalem. Many returned gladly. Many others, however, chose instead to remain in Persia or to move elsewhere.

Isaiah, who lived about seven hundred years before Jesus, shared God's message: "I will raise up Cyrus . . . he will rebuild my city and set my exiles free" (45:13)—more than a hundred years before it happened.

For most of the next six centuries, the situation in the Jewish homeland was far less glorious than the prophets had advertised. The Jewish people were dominated by a series of foreign powers—Persia, Greece, then Rome. In AD 70, more than three decades after the crucifixion of Jesus, the people of Judah rebelled against their Roman occupiers. Rome brutally crushed this uprising, destroying Jerusalem—including the temple—and precipitating another diaspora of the Jews.

For centuries, the descendants of Abraham settled here and there, carving out lives in far-flung places, establishing Jewish expatriate communities all over. Some continued to practice their faith—and ponder the ancient prophecies in the Hebrew scriptures. Others became irreligious, clinging only to their Jewish ethnic heritage.

Theodor Herzl (1860–1904), an Austro-Hungarian journalist, is known as the father of modern political Zionism—and of the modern State of Israel.

Fast-forward to the nineteenth and twentieth centuries. Europe was awash with anti-Semitism. This racial hostility sparked the Zionist movement, a grassroots effort among Jews to relocate to the land of their forefathers. When the British government issued the Balfour Declaration at the end of World War I, which called for the establishment of a permanent Jewish homeland in Palestine, a giant wave of Jewish immigration followed. Not surprisingly, this led to rising tensions between the Arabs already in the land

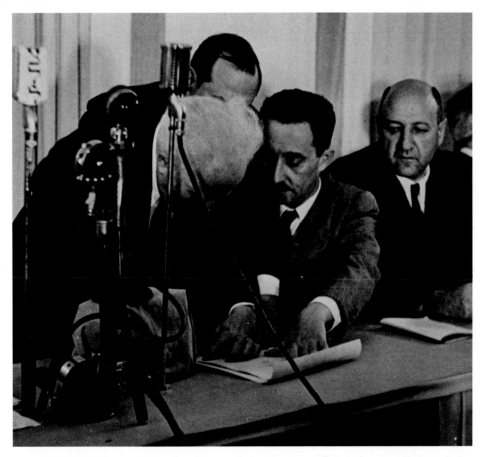

David Ben-Gurion, first president of modern Israel, signs the new nation's declaration of independence.

and all those Jewish newcomers. Great Britain tried, unsuccessfully, to broker peace between these factions throughout the 1920s and early 1930s. However, by the late 1930s, the British were much too distracted by Hitler's rise in Europe—and worried about the future of their own country—to focus on tiny Palestine.

Following World War II, other entities began working to resolve the Jewish-Arab conflict. The key moment came on November 29, 1947, when the fledgling United Nations voted to partition Palestine. This laid the groundwork for the political restoration of the Jewish State. Jews worldwide were elated; Arabs were furious. A vicious cycle of military attacks—and counterattacks—commenced.

THE MEANING OF ZION

Mount Zion is first mentioned in the Bible in 2 Samuel 5:7, where King David is said to have conquered the Jebusites who were holed up in a fortress they had built there. This explains why Jerusalem is sometimes called "the City of David." Later, the name *Zion* was used to refer to all of Jerusalem and then the entire region Judah. It is also used sometimes as a name for the people of Israel (Zechariah 9:13). Many psalms speak of God dwelling in Zion. Psalm 87 describes God's loyal love for Jerusalem and how He will look with special favor on those who were "born in Zion."

In the New Testament the word *Zion* is used to represent heaven, "the city of the living God, the heavenly Jerusalem" (Hebrews 12:22). In Zion, John prophesied, God will dwell with His people forever.

On May 14, 1948, Jewish leaders signed what essentially was a document of independence that declared Israel to be a sovereign state. War broke out the following day between the Jews and their Arab neighbors. In the seventy-plus years since, hostilities have never entirely ceased. Meanwhile, the number of Jews living in the land of Abraham, Isaac, and Jacob has continued to grow.

Many Bible scholars, teachers, and readers see these events as the initial fulfillments of numerous ancient prophecies that God would one day bring His people home.

THE ANCIENT PROPHECIES ABOUT ISRAEL BEING RESTORED

Careful Bible readers are quick to notice that God repeatedly promised through the prophets that He would regather His people and replant them in the land of their forefathers. To give an exhaustive list of verses here would be, well, exhausting; but consider this representative selection of passages.

After predicting the coming of the Messiah from Jesse's family, the prophet Isaiah wrote: "In that day the Lord will reach out his hand a second time to reclaim the surviving remnant of his people from Assyria, from Lower Egypt, from Upper Egypt, from Cush, from Elam, from Babylonia, from Hamath and from the islands of the Mediterranean. He will raise a banner for the nations and gather the exiles of Israel; he will assemble the scattered people of Judah from the four quarters of the earth" (Isaiah 11:11–12).

Later he prophesied, "Gather together and come; assemble, you fugitives from the nations" (Isaiah 45:20).

Isaiah prophesied of Israel, "The desert and the parched land will be glad; the wilderness will rejoice and blossom" (35:1).

"FROM THE WEST"

The prophet Hosea once declared, "'They will follow the LORD; he will roar like a lion. When he roars, his children will come trembling *from the west*. They will come from Egypt, trembling like sparrows, from Assyria, fluttering like doves. I will settle them in their homes,' declares the LORD" (Hosea 11:10–11, emphasis added).

The Israelites exiled to Assyria in 722 BC and Babylon between 605 and 586 BC would have returned to the Holy Land *from the east*. Thus, many believe this prophecy of Hosea about returnees coming *from the west* suggests a future regathering, when Jews will return to the Promised Land from Europe and the Americas. Many see the great flood of Jews to Israel in the last century as a partial fulfillment of such prophecies.

The prophet Jeremiah recorded this declaration of the Almighty:

"The days are coming," declares the LORD, "when I will raise up for David a righteous Branch, a King who will reign wisely and do what is just and right in the land. In his days Judah will be saved and Israel will live in safety. This is the name by which he will be called: The LORD Our Righteous Savior. So then, the days are coming," declares the LORD, "when people will no longer say, 'As surely as the LORD lives, who brought the Israelites up out of Egypt,' but they will say, 'As surely as the LORD lives, who brought the descendants of Israel up out of the land of the north and out of all the countries where he had banished them.' Then they will live in their own land." (Jeremiah 23:5–8)

Elsewhere, Jeremiah wrote:

"So do not be afraid, Jacob my servant; do not be dismayed, Israel," declares the LORD. "I will surely save you out of a distant place, your descendants from the land of their exile. Jacob will again have peace and security, and no one will make him afraid. I am with you and will save you," declares the LORD. "Though I completely destroy all the nations among which I scatter you, I will not completely destroy you. I will discipline you but only in due measure; I will not let you go entirely unpunished." (Jeremiah 30:10–11; see also Jeremiah 46:27)

Here's what God had to say through the prophet Ezekiel about a future regathering of His people:

"'Although I sent them far away among the nations and scattered them among the countries, yet for a little while I have been a sanctuary for them in the countries where they have gone. . . . I will gather you from the nations and bring you back from the countries where you have been scattered, and I will give you back the land of Israel again.'

"They will return to it and remove all its vile images and detestable idols. I will give them an undivided heart and put a new spirit in them; I will remove from them their heart of stone and give them a heart of flesh. Then they will follow my decrees and be careful to keep my laws. They will be my people, and I will be their God." (Ezekiel 11:16–20; see also 39:25–29)

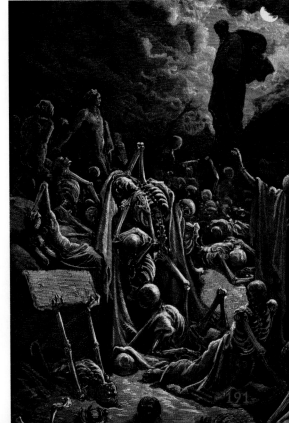

Ezekiel sees a valley of dry bones restored to life—an image of the restoration of the Jewish people.

In Ezekiel's best-known vision, he sees a valley full of dry bones come together and return to life. In that vision, God tells him, "Son of man, these bones are the people of Israel. They say, 'Our bones are dried up and our hope is gone; we are cut off.' Therefore prophesy and say to them: 'This is what the Sovereign LORD says: My people, I am going to open your graves and bring you up from them; I will bring you back to the land of Israel. Then you, my people, will know that I am the LORD, when I open your graves and bring you up from them. I will put my Spirit in you and you will live, and I will settle you in your own land. Then you will know that I the LORD have spoken, and I have done it, declares the LORD'" (Ezekiel 37:11–14).

Zephaniah, one of the minor prophets, was also given a stunning glimpse of Israel's glorious future.

Sing, Daughter Zion; shout aloud, Israel! Be glad and rejoice with all your heart, Daughter Jerusalem! The LORD has taken away your punishment, he has turned back your enemy. The LORD, the King of Israel, is with you; never again will you fear

WHAT IS *ALIYAH*?

The Hebrew word *aliyah* means "ascent." This is the word used to describe the voluntary immigration of scattered Jews back to the land of Israel. A Jew who moves back to Israel is said to be "making aliyah" or engaging in "the act of going up." Because of the nation's "law of return," Jews making aliyah have an automatic right to Israeli citizenship.

Those who have a dispensational approach to interpreting scripture believe the end times will involve a mass return of Jews to Israel, as per the many prophecies about God regathering His people. Some see recent events as evidence of this, including the establishment of the State of Israel in 1948. Since then, more than three million Jews have returned to their ancestral homeland.

Tents serve as temporary housing for European Jews moving into Israel following the horrors of World War II.

any harm. On that day they will say to Jerusalem, "Do not fear, Zion; do not let your hands hang limp. The LORD your God is with you, the Mighty Warrior who saves. He will take great delight in you; in his love he will no longer rebuke you, but will rejoice over you with singing.... At that time I will gather you; at that time I will bring you home. I will give you honor and praise among all the peoples of the earth when I restore your fortunes before your very eyes," says the LORD. (Zephaniah 3:14–17, 20)

Most conservative scholars agree that all these prophecies were given before 538 BC. Therefore, many argue that these ancient predictions were fulfilled, at least partially, when the Jewish exiles returned home from Babylonian captivity. Most, however, see details in these assorted visions that never materialized in the past, predictions that remain unfulfilled. The prophets speak of a regathering that seems to transcend the events that happened in 538 BC when Cyrus told the exiled Jews to go home. The proponents of this view say that this is more than a return from Babylonia; it's "from the four quarters of the earth" (Isaiah 11:12). As such, many look to a future outworking of these predictions.

FOUR VIEWS ON ISRAEL'S FUTURE

All Christians agree that Israel has a future and some sort of role in God's prophetic plan. However, believers sometimes disagree and argue about what the prophets meant when they spoke about a future "Israel."

Some interpret Bible passages like those cited above as referring to an ethnic Israel, a distinct political entity. Others understand "Israel" in a metaphorical or spiritual sense. Within these two camps are four different ways of understanding Israel's future. We could label these (1) covenant theology; (2) replacement theology—also

The flag of modern Israel flies over the old city of Jerusalem.

known as "supersessionism"; (3) classical dispensationalism; and (4) progressive dispensationalism. What are the particular nuances of each view?

Covenant theology, as mentioned in an earlier chapter, teaches that God has operated in history by different covenant agreements with humanity. Adherents of this view see, at minimum, two covenants: one of works and one of grace. Covenant theologians believe there is an uninterrupted progression from the Old to the New Testament. They see a single objective for God's chosen people, also known as "the elect." They don't distinguish between Old Testament saints (Israel) and New Testament believers (the church). They see all God's faithful followers as belonging to the same community. Due to this understanding, they regard the ancient promises made to Israel in the Old Testament as relevant to the church today. "Israel," according to covenant theology, is all the people of God, including modern-day Christians.

This understanding leads covenant theologians to conclude that Old Testaments prophecies about the restoration of Israel have now been fulfilled—and even expanded—in Christ. The original prophecies regarding a literal piece of land are now seen as predictions about God's spiritual and eternal kingdom, and about the renewal and restoration of all creation. In this view, one doesn't have to be a physical descendant of Abraham to experience the blessings foretold by the prophets. They are for anyone and everyone who is faithful to God. And so, perhaps all those promises about Israel's return simply refer to people coming to God in their hearts.

Replacement theology, or supersessionism, says that because the nation of Israel refused to embrace Jesus as Messiah at His first advent, the promises made to Abraham's physical descendants were rescinded and transferred to the church. In this way of thinking, Israel is no longer God's chosen people—the church is. It is the new Israel, having replaced or superseded Israel in God's redemptive plan.

How then do adherents of this view read the promises given to Abraham and his descendants? They see prophecies of Israel's future restoration as promises of blessing for modern-day Christians. They see the Mosaic covenant (Exodus 20) as having been replaced by the new covenant (Luke 22:20). Thus, there is no future divine plan for a literal, ethnically homogenous State of Israel.

Dispensationalism comes in two varieties: classical and progressive. The word *dispensation* (see Ephesians 1:10; 3:2; Colossians 1:25 in the Authorized Version) is the Greek word *oikonomia*, which means "stewardship" or "administration." This is the word from which we get our English term *economy*. Dispensationalism basically says that the world functions like a big household run by God. Through the ages, God has administrated or managed His household via distinct plans at different times. According to the late theologian Charles C. Ryrie, a dispensation is "a distinguishable economy in the outworking of God's purpose."[1]

Practically speaking, in trying to understand God's plan, dispensationalists maintain a clear distinction between Israel and the church. Classical dispensationalists view the present era as a sort of parenthetical break in God's ultimate plan for Israel. Progressive dispensationalists, on the other hand, see the current church age

PAUL AND THE FUTURE OF ISRAEL

The "Jewish credentials" of Saul—later more famously known as Paul—were impeccable. He was "circumcised on the eighth day, of the people of Israel, of the tribe of Benjamin, a Hebrew of Hebrews; in regard to the law, a Pharisee" (Philippians 3:5). Thus when Paul first heard the "good news" that the followers of Jesus were announcing around Jerusalem, he didn't consider it good news at all. Jesus, a rabble-rousing carpenter from Nazareth, could not possibly be Israel's Messiah. Jesus rising from the dead? Paul wasn't buying any of it. In fact, he was furious and set out to crush this new movement. The only problem? The resurrected Jesus unexpectedly appeared to him. In a flash, this great enemy of the Christian faith became its biggest advocate (see Acts 9).

For the rest of his life, everywhere he went, Paul pleaded with his fellow Jews to accept Jesus as their Messiah. A few heeded his pleas; most did not. In a long letter to the Christians living in Rome, Paul talked extensively of God's plan for the Jewish people.

Speaking of the Jewish rejection of Christ, he wrote: "Again I ask: Did they stumble so as to fall beyond recovery? Not at all! Rather, because of their transgression, salvation has come to the Gentiles to make Israel envious. But if their transgression means riches for the world, and their loss means riches for the Gentiles, how much greater riches will their full inclusion bring!" (Romans 11:11–12).

as a continuation of, not an interruption in, God's redemptive plan. Both camps agree that at some unknown point in the future, God will again focus His attention on Israel.

All this means that dispensationalists—unlike proponents of replacement theology—do not believe the church has replaced Israel in God's plan. Unlike covenant theologians, dispensationalists are careful not to apply the Old Testament promises made to Israel to the church. On the contrary, they interpret all those Old Testament prophecies about Israel once again flourishing in the Promised Land and being a blessing to the nations as literal and unconditional (Jeremiah 16:14–15; 23:8; 29:14; 30:3; 32:37). To bolster their case, they point to passages such as Romans 9–11.

Dispensationalists understand these verses to suggest that when the Jews did not accept their Messiah, God unveiled a previously hidden mystery: the church age. This would result in countless Gentiles coming to faith in Israel's God through Christ (see Ephesians 3).

Some look at all this religious history—Judaism giving birth to Christianity—and say that the church has now *replaced* Israel in God's plan. However, in verse 12, Paul speaks of "their full inclusion." The significant Greek word in this phrase is the word *pleroma*, which means "full number" or "full measure" or "completion." In ancient Greek works other than the Bible, the word was used to describe a ship with a full crew. Many think Paul's use of this term means that Israel's "fall" is only temporary—that a future regathering and restoration of national Israel awaits.

The apostle Paul, depicted here in prison by the seventeenth-century Dutch master Rembrandt, once wrote, "I could wish that I myself were cursed and cut off from Christ for the sake of my people, those of my own race, the people of Israel" (Romans 9:3–4).

Specifically, Romans 11:1 says, "I ask then: Did God reject his people? By no means!" This is seen as irrefutable evidence that God has a future for ethnic Israel.

This probably explains why dispensationalists tend to be highly supportive of the modern State of Israel. Many see the establishment of the Jewish state in 1948 as a beginning to the fulfillment of biblical prophecy regarding God's ancient people. For them, the survival of the Jews during centuries of persecution and near genocide is proof of God's faithfulness (Jeremiah 31:36).

THE IMPORTANCE OF THE TEMPLE AND MOUNT MORIAH

King David had a deep desire to build a magnificent temple for God. However, God told David that his son would complete this great project (1 Chronicles 22:9–10). The final chapters of 1 Chronicles describe the royal effort to gather the necessary building supplies. In the early chapters of 2 Chronicles we read: "Then Solomon began to

The golden-topped Muslim Dome of the Rock is currently the most visible feature of the Temple Mount.

build the temple of the LORD in Jerusalem on Mount Moriah, where the LORD had appeared to his father David. It was on the threshing floor of Araunah the Jebusite, the place provided by David" (3:1).

Why is this building site so significant? Mount Moriah was—as 2 Chronicles 3:1 says—where David bought a threshing floor from Araunah, built an altar, made sacrifices, and prayed for an end to the deadly plague that God had sent on Israel when David conducted an unauthorized military census (see 2 Samuel 24:21). Mount Moriah is also where the Jews, upon returning to Jerusalem from their days of exile in Babylon, rebuilt the Jewish temple under Zerubbabel's leadership. Centuries later, Herod enlarged and refurbished this structure, and it became known as Herod's temple. This was the temple during the time of Christ, which the Romans destroyed in AD 70.

As of this writing, all that remains of Herod's temple is part of a retaining wall known as the Western Wall or the Wailing Wall. In AD 685, Muslims built a mosque, the Dome of the Rock, on the site.

Due to prophetic visions, some believe a new Jewish temple must be built—and will be built—on Mount Moriah in the future.

What visions of the prophets are we talking about? Here are a few examples.

From the prophecies of Isaiah: "This is what Isaiah son of Amoz saw concerning Judah and Jerusalem: In the last days the mountain of the LORD's temple will be established as the highest of the mountains; it will be exalted above the hills, and all nations will stream to it. Many peoples will come and say, 'Come, let us go up to the mountain of the LORD, to the temple of the God of Jacob. He will teach us his ways, so that we may walk in his paths.' The law will go out from Zion, the word of the LORD from Jerusalem" (Isaiah 2:1–3).

From the prophecies of Ezekiel: Chapter 40 of his book begins, "In the twenty-fifth year of our exile ... the hand of the LORD was on me and he took me there" (verse 1). For several chapters, the prophet described being taken in a vision to the city of Jerusalem and being given a comprehensive tour of a future temple. His tour guide was a "man whose appearance was like bronze" (verse 3), which probably means he was an angel. When the man brought him to the gate facing east, Ezekiel wrote:

> I saw the glory of the God of Israel coming from the east. His voice was like the roar of rushing waters, and the land was radiant with his glory ... and I fell facedown. The glory of the LORD entered the temple through the gate facing east. Then the Spirit lifted me up and brought me into the inner court, and the glory of the LORD filled the temple. While the man was standing beside me, I heard someone speaking to me from inside the temple. He said: "Son of man, this is the place of my throne and the place for the soles of my feet. This is where I will live among the Israelites forever." (Ezekiel 43:1–7)

What temple was Ezekiel seeing in this strange and detailed vision? Some say it was the temple rebuilt after

A reconstruction of first-century Jerusalem, highlighted by Herod's Temple at the center. Prophecy experts debate exactly which temple—historical or future—is described in Ezekiel's prophecies.

the exile and later revamped by Herod. Other say all this "temple talk" is figurative and symbolic of invisible spiritual realities. Dispensational Christians believe that there is no way to square the temple Ezekiel saw in his visions (see Ezekiel 40–44) with the temple rebuilt by the exiles or with Herod's temple. They argue, therefore, that Ezekiel's temple must be a literal temple to be rebuilt in the future on Mount Moriah (where the Islamic Dome of the Rock now sits). In their view, this temple will be the center of worldwide worship when Jesus returns to establish His earthly kingdom.

From the prophecies of Micah:

In the last days the mountain of the LORD's temple will be established as the highest of the mountains; it will be exalted above the hills, and peoples will stream to it.

Many nations will come and say, "Come, let us go up to the mountain of the LORD, to the temple of the God of Jacob. He will teach us his ways, so that we may walk in his paths." The law will go out from Zion, the word of the LORD from Jerusalem. He will judge between many peoples and will settle disputes for strong nations far and wide. They will beat their swords into plowshares and their spears into pruning hooks. Nation will not take up sword against nation, nor will they train for war anymore....

"In that day," declares the LORD, "I will gather the lame; I will assemble the exiles and those I have brought to grief. I will make the lame my remnant, those driven away a strong nation. The LORD will rule over them in Mount Zion from that day and forever." (Micah 4:1–3, 6–7)

A statue outside the United Nations building in New York City commemorates Micah's prophecy of a day when the nations "will beat their swords into plowshares and their spears into pruning hooks" (4:3).

MILLENNIAL REIGN OF CHRIST

When we speak of the millennial reign of Christ, we're not talking about "millennial" Christians born between 1981 and 1997 (also known as Generation Y). The millennial reign of Christ is the label given to something described in Revelation 20:2–7. Six times in that passage, John mentioned a thousand-year period. He also described the martyrs of the tribulation reigning with Christ (verse 4).

Jesus as king of the world, from a Viennese church fresco.

Some interpret the "thousand years" allegorically. They see this phrase as a symbolic or figurative way of implying "a really long period of time." In this view, Bible readers should not expect a literal, physical, earthly reign of Jesus. Others see this millennial reign of Christ as an actual thousand-year period in the future. They believe that upon Christ's return to earth, He will establish Himself as earth's true King from Zion. He will rule there from David's throne (Luke 1:32–33).

We'll talk more about these views in the next chapter.

In this vision of a glorious future Zion, Micah used almost the same phraseology as we find in Isaiah 2. He pictured the temple complete and functioning. He described a city, nation, and world at peace. Many would say that he and the other prophets were describing the millennial kingdom or reign of Christ.

OUR SWORDS INTO PLOWSHARES

As we think about these prophetic passages regarding the future of the Jewish people and the Promised Land, what conclusions can we draw? As we've seen in this chapter, that depends on how we interpret and define the term *Israel*.

But while we're wrestling with that, here are some things every believer should agree on:

✳ To be thankful today for how God has worked in history through the children of Abraham to reveal Himself to the world

✳ To stand against anti-Semitism in every ugly form it presents itself

✳ To "pray for the peace of Jerusalem" (Psalm 122:6)

ENDNOTES

1   Charles C. Ryrie, *Dispensationalism Today* (Chicago: Moody Press, 1965), 29.

Chapter 9:

TWENTY QUESTIONS ABOUT THE END OF THE WORLD

Before video games and the Internet, the game Twenty Questions was a quaint way kids entertained themselves on long road trips and boring rainy days. Someone would think of an object, person, or event—for example, a black horse—and the others would take turns asking yes-or-no questions to narrow down the possibilities and figure out the correct answer.

In this chapter we're going to adapt that game to try to figure out what the Bible says about the end of the world. We'll ask twenty

THE MEANING OF *ESCHATOLOGY*

Our word *eschatology* comes from two Greek words: the adjective *eschatos*, which means "last," and the suffix *-logy*, meaning "the study of." Put them together and you get *eschatology*, the study of last things, or events at the end of the world. This fascinating branch of theology involves analyzing what the Bible says about the return of Christ and other controversial topics such as the rapture, the tribulation, the millennium, the final judgment, heaven, and hell. What is the fate of Satan and demons? Of earth? Of the Jewish state? All these topics and more are what we mean when we speak of *eschatology*.

Christians sometimes think they need not study eschatology, concluding that it is too complex for the average person. However, when we use sound, consistent principles of interpretation, eschatology becomes understandable and inspirational. It can help us to align our lives now with things to come.

common questions people have about the end times, questions often sparked by reading the book of Revelation. Reader alert: the answers we discover will be more involved than a simple yes or no.

QUESTION #1: WHY STUDY THE BOOK OF REVELATION?

Near the end of the first century, John—most say the *apostle* John— was exiled on the island of Patmos in the Mediterranean Sea. There he received and wrote down a wild, apocalyptic vision. The result is what we know as the book of Revelation. (Note: the title of the book is singular—Revelation, not Revelations.)

Domitian was the Roman emperor at the time. He was a brutal, vain ruler who demanded to be worshiped as a god. Those who refused—mostly the Christians in the empire—were routinely thrown in prison, sent into exile, tortured, or executed.

John's revelation offered hope for those suffering believers. It was a bracing reminder of God's sovereignty and faithfulness. And it prophesied the ultimate triumph of the church. But is that all John's vision was intended to be? Encouragement for perse-cuted believers in the late first and early second centuries? Many Bible scholars say an emphatic *no*. They argue that the events John described ultimately point to the end of the world and beyond—primarily because of what John was commanded to do: "Write, therefore, what you have seen, what is now and *what will take place later*" (Revelation 1:19, emphasis added).

As we've been saying all along, a significant portion of the Bible is prophetic. The Old Testament prophets spoke emphatically of future things. Jesus told His followers to look for signs that would sig-nal His return (Matthew 24; Luke 13). Other apostles, such

In a relief from a monastery in Toledo, Spain, the apostle John writes the revelation of Jesus Christ.

as Paul, used their letters to educate believers about coming reali-ties (1 Thessalonians 4:15–17; 2 Thessalonians 2:1–15). Since the famous and controversial book of Revelation sits at the end of the New Testament, and since it was—in the opinion of some scholars—the final book of scripture to be written, Revelation can be seen as the consummation of all the Old and New Testament prophecies.

This "revelation from Jesus Christ" (Revelation 1:1) begins with a tantalizing offer: "Blessed is the one who reads aloud the words of this prophecy, and blessed are those who hear it and take to heart what is written in it, because the time is near" (Revelation 1:3). It ends with a dire warning: "And if anyone takes words away from this scroll of prophecy, God will take away from that person any share in the tree of life and in the Holy City, which are described in this scroll" (Revelation 22:19).

Though it's tempting to study only the parts of the Bible that make us feel good, or the books that are straightforward and relatively easy to interpret, we have to remember that "all Scripture is God-breathed" (2 Timothy 3:16). And, since John's Revelation is, by its own description, all about Jesus, anyone who wants to know Him has no choice but to dig in.

QUESTION #2: HOW DO WE MAKE SENSE OF THE BIBLE'S FINAL BOOK?

People tend to interpret the book of Revelation in one of four ways. We know these as the historicist, preterist, idealist, and futurist views.

THE HISTORICIST VIEW OF REVELATION
Historicism is an eschatological, or end-times, interpretive approach that teaches as follows:

* The events described in Revelation are representative of the major events of church history, from the time of John until the end of the age.
* The seven churches in Revelation 2–3 represent different eras in church history.
* The symbols and figures in Revelation stand for actual historical people and events—although there is little consensus about what exactly the symbols symbolize.
* Except for the return of Christ and the eternal estate, most of the events described in Revelation have already occurred in history.

Ruins of ancient Ephesus, location of one of the seven churches highlighted in Revelation, which factor heavily into the "historicist" interpretation of the book.

The historicist view was very popular during the Reformation (1517–1648). It is not held by many today.

THE PRETERIST VIEW OF REVELATION

The preterist view espouses these ideas:

❋ The book of Revelation was written *before* AD 70, *not* in the late first century.

❋ The cataclysmic events Revelation describes (and that Jesus prophesied in Matthew 24) were fulfilled historically—specifically in the first century when the Romans decimated Jerusalem in AD 70.

✻ John was addressing the real issues of real churches (see Revelation 2–3) that existed at that time; he was *not* writing about the end times. He wrote primarily to encourage believers to continue in the faith despite official state persecution.

✻ Israel finds its continuation or fulfillment in the church; there is no distinction between Jew and Gentile.

✻ Jesus' second coming has already happened in a spiritual sense; this is the belief of full preterists, whereas partial preterists hold that it has not yet taken place.

✻ Because Revelation's prophecies were fulfilled in the last century, the book cannot be about the future.

The highly symbolic (if not bizarre) imagery of Revelation leads some to call for a figurative interpretation of the entire book. Here, a dragon is shown spitting out a flood to try to destroy "the woman who had given birth to the male child" (12:13).

THE IDEALIST VIEW OF REVELATION

The idealist view advocates this way of understanding the book:

✳ Because Revelation is apocalyptic literature containing heavy symbolic imagery, the book should be interpreted figuratively.

✳ It is merely a non-historical vision of various spiritual realities.

✳ Its messages are not limited to a particular historical era; they do not point to specific socio-political events. For example, the battles described in Revelation symbolize the ongoing battle between good and evil, the persecution of believers, or simply human warfare in general; they are not predictive of specific future battles.

✳ We should read the imagery in Revelation as an encouragement to live a holy life here and now in an unholy, often hostile culture.

The idealist view is often associated with *amillennialism* (see question 16). In this view, the thousand-year reign of Christ described in Revelation 20 is symbolic rather than literal. In other words, Christians reign with Christ as they strive to bring about justice and righteousness in the world. Or perhaps they see the reign of Christ as spiritual in nature, meaning that Jesus is enthroned in the hearts of His followers and not physically sitting on an actual future throne on earth.

THE FUTURIST VIEW OF REVELATION

The futurist view sees John's book from this standpoint:

* ✳ Despite being apocalyptic literature, Revelation is meant to be interpreted in the most straightforward, literal sense possible; thus, we should take into account all lexical, grammatical, and historical evidence.
* ✳ The book contains an "outline" in its first chapter: "'Write, therefore, what you have seen, what is now and what will take place later'" (Revelation 1:19). Chapter 1 describes the past ("what you have seen"). Chapters 2–3 describe the present ("what is now"). Chapters 4–22 spell out events yet to be fulfilled ("what will take place later"). Revelation, then, is primarily about events to come. It looks toward the end of the world.
* ✳ The Lord's return will occur in two stages: Jesus will come for His church (an event known as the rapture); and He will come back with His church in glorious power to conquer His enemies and establish His kingdom.

The futurist view is most closely associated with dispensationalism. This is the theological idea that says God never has and never will change (Malachi 3:6); however, He has at key points in history changed the way He deals with humankind. For example, in the Old Testament, God chose and formed Israel to be a light to the world. But when the Jewish nation rejected Jesus as its Messiah, God set Israel aside for a time and established the church to be a light to the world. Futurists—or dispensationalists—see the current era of the church as a parenthesis in history, bracketed by God's dealings with Israel on either side. For dispensationalists, promises made *to* Israel in the Old Testament are *for* Israel. They should not be spiritualized or applied to the church. Futurists believe God will make good on all those prophecies that speak of Israel flourishing in the Promised Land and Christ reigning from a throne on Mount Zion.

QUESTION #3: WHAT IS APOSTASY?

When speaking about the coming "day of the Lord"—see question 12 below—the apostle Paul wrote these chilling words: "Don't let anyone deceive you in any way, for that day will not come until the rebellion occurs and the man of lawlessness is revealed, the man doomed to destruction" (2 Thessalonians 2:3).

The Greek word translated as "rebellion" is *apostasia*. It means "to fall away" or "to revolt against authority."

Paul used it to speak of renouncing or abandoning the Christian faith that one previously espoused. One claims to be a follower of Jesus and is therefore considered faithful; but then one abandons that faith and is regarded as faithless. Verses such as 2 Thessalonians 2:3 suggest that in the last days,

A derelict church building hints at the meaning of *apostasy*—an abandoning of the faith.

213

just before the day of the Lord, we will see wide-scale apostasy, an exodus of so-called believers from churches. Many think this will be the prelude for the arrival of the "the man of lawlessness"—that is, the Antichrist (see question 13).

QUESTION #4: WHAT DOES THE BIBLE MEAN REGARDING "THE TIMES OF THE GENTILES"?

From start to finish, the Bible shows God expressing His love and concern for people of "every nation, tribe, language and people" (Revelation 14:6). Even though the Old Testament focuses primarily on Israel's part in God's redemptive plan, there's an emphasis on Gentile salvation, too (see the book of Jonah, for example).

In Luke 21, Jesus prophesied about Jerusalem being "trampled on by the Gentiles until the times of the Gentiles are fulfilled" (verse

While most Jews have rejected Jesus as Messiah, many Gentiles have accepted Him—and today, many visit the land of His life and work.

24). In Romans 11, the apostle Paul spoke similarly about the Jews experiencing a spiritual "hardening in part until the full number of the Gentiles has come in" (verse 25). What do these verses mean?

We don't find these exact phrases in the Old Testament, but we do find many references and allusions to Gentile domination of the world and of Israel. This would occur before the return of the King of kings, Jesus the Messiah.

In his letters, Paul explained that God opened the way for Gentiles to come to faith in Jesus; indeed, this was the major focus of Paul's missionary efforts. However, the Almighty was by no means finished with the Jewish people (see Romans 9–11). The hardening of the Jewish nation was only temporary. In Paul's ministry individual Jews *did* believe in Jesus (and others would continue to do so throughout history), but the nation as a whole would not embrace Jesus as Messiah until God's purposes for the Gentiles were fulfilled. Then Paul declared that at God's appointed time, "all Israel will be saved" (Romans 11:26). The prophet Zechariah said it like this: "They will look on . . . the one they have pierced, and they will mourn" (Zechariah 12:10). And so God's plan to bless all nations—Jewish and Gentile—will be fulfilled, exactly as promised.

QUESTION #5: WHAT ABOUT THE RAPTURE?

Surely you've heard people speak about the rapture. If so, you know this is one of the most hotly debated subjects in the field of eschatology. Much of the tension is due to the fact that the word *rapture* is not found in the Bible. Here's the passage that's the catalyst for most of the controversy:

> For we believe that Jesus died and rose again, and so we believe that God will bring with Jesus those who have fallen asleep in him. According to the Lord's word, we tell you that we who are

still alive, who are left until the coming of the Lord, will certainly not precede those who have fallen asleep. For the Lord himself will come down from heaven, with a loud command, with the voice of the archangel and with the trumpet call of God, and the dead in Christ will rise first. After that, we who are still alive and are left will be caught up together with them in the clouds to meet the Lord in the air. And so we will be with the Lord forever. (1 Thessalonians 4:14–17)

Paul wrote that at "the coming of the Lord," the "dead in Christ will rise first." Then believers "who are still alive" will be "caught up . . . to meet the Lord in the air." The verb *caught up* is a translation of the Greek word *harpázô*, which means "to snatch up" or "take away." When the Bible was translated into Latin, translators rendered this idea of being snatched up with the word *rapturo*. That's where we get our English term *rapture*.

The "voice of the archangel and . . . the trumpet call of God" (1 Thessalonians 4:16) will touch off an event that many call the rapture.

Paul wrote these words to comfort concerned members in the church at Thessalonica, Greece. They were essentially asking, "What about our Christian friends who have already died? Since they're dead, won't they miss out on Christ's return?"

Paul gave these believers an order of events: When Christ comes, the dead will be resurrected first, then those still alive will be caught up together with them. The reason? "To meet the Lord in the air." The result? To be "with the Lord forever" (see also 1 Thessalonians 5:10).

Some have pointed out that the language Paul used in this passage mirrors the way ancient people welcomed a visiting dignitary. A herald would sound a trumpet announcing the VIP's arrival. Then the citizens of the city would go out, meet their esteemed visitor, and escort him back to the city (see, for example, Acts 28:15). Many understand Paul's words here as saying that believers will be caught up to meet Jesus in the air and later accompany Him—with His angelic armies—when He returns to earth.

When *in the end-times sequence of events*—not the day, date, and year—will the rapture occur? It depends on how one understands the events known as the millennium (see question 16) and the tribulation (see question 11). There are several views.

Premillennialism teaches that the rapture will happen *before* a literal thousand-year reign of Christ (Revelation 20:4–7) on the earth; however, there is no consensus about when the rapture will happen in relation to the tribulation. Most argue that all true believers will be raptured by Christ *before* the beginning of a terrible seven-year period of tribulation and suffering. This is called the "pretribulation" perspective. Others think the rapture will happen in the *middle* of this seven-year time of tribulation. This is known as the "mid-tribulation" perspective. Still others hold to what it known as historic-premillenialism. They are convinced the rapture will occur at the *end* of the seven-year tribulation.

Amillenialists believe the thousand-year reign described in Revelation 20 is symbolic and not to be interpreted literally. *Postmillennialists* believe the second coming will take place *after* a millennial era. Neither group views the rapture as a separate event from Christ's second coming. The rapture and second coming of Christ are, according to these groups, one and the same.

One of the biggest issues raised by this discussion is this question: Would a good God allow His faithful people to suffer? Of course, we know from scripture (John 16:33; Acts 14:22), from history, and from personal experience that the answer is yes. Christians are never promised an exemption from suffering—only that God will be with them in it and see them through it.

QUESTION #6: WHEN WILL CHRIST RETURN?

Near the end of His life, Jesus predicted the destruction of the temple (Matthew 24:1–2). This sparked a flurry of questions from the disciples. "When will this happen, and what will be the sign of your coming and of the end of the age?" (Matthew 24:3).

These are the same questions Christians have wrestled with for almost two thousand years. Every now and then a self-proclaimed Bible expert will come out of the woodwork with "the answer." Obviously

William Miller gained fame in the nineteenth century for his prediction that Jesus would return around 1843. He is one of many whose forecasts proved inaccurate.

218

these individuals aren't real prophets, because the specific dates they announce for Christ's return always come and go uneventfully.

The short answer to the question *When will Christ return?* is "Only God knows." Jesus told His followers, "But about that day or hour no one knows, not even the angels in heaven, nor the Son, but only the Father" (Matthew 24:36). In light of that, the Bible urges believers to be watchful, to live with a sense of imminence and readiness.

QUESTION #7: WHAT ARE THE SIGNS FOR CHRIST'S RETURN?

No preacher, teacher, or Bible scholar knows *precisely* when Jesus will return. This is why the Lord said, "The Son of Man will come at an hour when you do not expect him" (Matthew 24:44). However, the apostle Paul suggested it's still possible to be prepared. He urged, "But you, brothers and sisters, are not in darkness so that this day should surprise you like a thief. You are all children of the light and children of the day. We do not belong to the night or to the darkness. So then, let us not be like others, who are asleep, but let us be awake and sober" (1 Thessalonians 5:4–6).

The reason Christians don't have to be surprised by the return of Christ is that Jesus gave His followers a list of signs to look for—unmistakable indicators that the end of the age is drawing near. In the Olivet Discourse (Matthew 24–25), He spoke of the following signs:

1. **International/Political Signs.** Specifically, Jesus mentioned "wars and rumors of wars" (Matthew 24:6), which some interpret as global conflicts, such as the world witnessed in World Wars I and II. Based on other prophetic passages, some also anticipate a kind of revived Roman Empire—from which the Antichrist will emerge (see Daniel 2:41–44; 7:7, 23–24; Revelation 17:12–13).

"Wars and rumors of wars" (Matthew 24:6) and an "increase of wickedness" (Matthew 24:12) are two signs pointing to Jesus' return to earth.

Dispensationalists add, "Don't forget about Israel!" They argue that the sudden creation of the Israeli state in 1948 was an important sign that the end is likely closer than we think.

2. **Signs in the Natural World.** Jesus told His followers to watch for earthquakes, famine, pestilence, and signs from heaven (Matthew 24:7; Luke 21:11). Are such things increasing in our day? Some wonder if climate change—whether or not it is caused or exacerbated by humans—is one such sign.

3. **Societal Signs.** Jesus spoke of a world marked by "the increase of wickedness" (Matthew 24:12). Some interpret this verse as describing life on earth during the still-future period of the tribulation. Perhaps so, but elsewhere Paul described the "last days"

as being characterized by the love of self, the love of money, and the love of pleasure (2 Timothy 3:1–5). Who would argue that such depictions don't apply to contemporary culture?

4. **Spiritual Signs:** Jesus spoke of the rise of false messiahs (Matthew 24:5, 11), the persecution of believers (Matthew 24:9), apostasy within the church (Matthew 24:24; 1 Timothy 4:1), and the continuing spread of the Gospel (Matthew 24:14).

Jesus said in Luke 21:28, "When these things begin to take place, stand up and lift up your heads, because your redemption is drawing near."

QUESTION #8: WHO ARE THE 144,000 IN REVELATION?

In Revelation 14, John wrote of seeing 144,000 men with Christ on Mount Zion singing a song "no one could learn" (verse 3). They are described as redeemed, honest, and sexually pure (verses 1–5; see also Revelation 7:1–8). Readers of Revelation naturally ask, "What is this group? Who are these people?"

As we would expect, views differ according to the interpretational approach one embraces when studying Revelation.

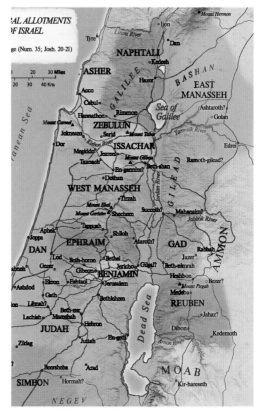

Revelation 7:3–8 indicates the 144,000 are 12,000 from each of the twelve tribes of Israel. Christians today debate whether this description is literal or figurative.

Those who take either the preterist or idealist view understand the 144,000 to symbolically represent the church. They take this 144,000 not literally but as signifying all redeemed people. Anyone who is a servant of God (Revelation 7:3) is considered one of the 144,000.

In contrast, the futurist sees 144,000 as a literal number: 12,000 men from each of the tribes of Israel. They see Romans 9–11 as evidence that the church has not replaced Israel, that each group has a distinctive role to play in the future

Regardless of which interpretation one accepts, the role of the 144,000 is clear. John suggested their assignment will be to take the Gospel to the world just before the end of the world. Because of their obedience, John wrote about seeing "a great multitude that no one could count, from every nation, tribe, people and language, standing before the throne and before the Lamb" (Revelation 7:9).

QUESTION #9: WHO ARE THE TWO WITNESSES?

In Revelation 11:1–2, John described a grim period lasting 1,260 days, or three and a half years, in which the Gentiles "will trample on the holy city." Next he introduced his readers to two figures clothed in sackcloth and appointed to prophesy for 1,260 days and call people to return to God. The apostle John referred to them as "two witnesses," "two olive trees," and "two lampstands" (Revelation

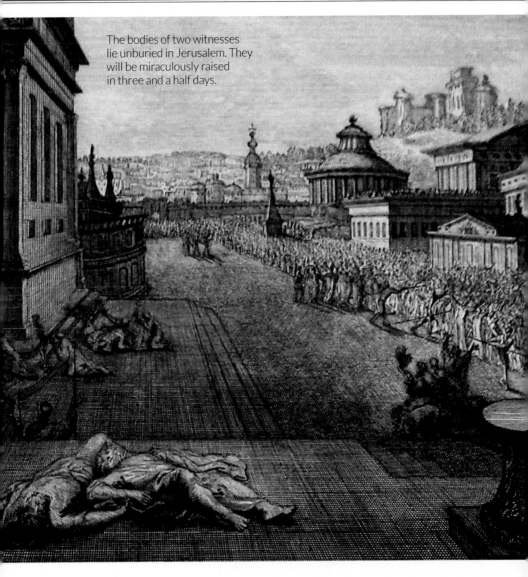

The bodies of two witnesses lie unburied in Jerusalem. They will be miraculously raised in three and a half days.

11:3–4), a description that sounds remarkably similar to what the Old Testament prophet Zechariah wrote (Zechariah 4:2–3, 14).

John continued, "If anyone tries to harm them, fire comes from their mouths and devours their enemies. This is how anyone who wants to harm them must die. They have power to shut up the heavens so that it will not rain during the time they are prophesying; and they have power to turn the waters into blood and to strike the earth with every kind of plague as often as they want" (Revelation 11:5–6).

John wrote that after the two witnesses' days of prophesying are over, the beast—see questions 13 and 14—will kill them (Revelation 11:7), precipitating a worldwide celebration. But three and a half days later, they will come back to life.

Who are these two witnesses? Some speculate they are just two ordinary believers who will be alive in the last days. Others have suggested the two witnesses symbolize two groups of people—Jews

"Doubting Thomas" inspects the wound in Jesus' side after His return to physical life. Jesus' resurrection would pave the way for the ultimate resurrection of everyone who follows Him.

and Gentiles. Still others believe these two figures are Moses and Elijah—because those two Old Testament saints did the same kinds of miracles these witnesses are described as doing (see Exodus 7:14–25; 1 Kings 17–18; 2 Kings 1). Others posit they are Enoch and Elijah—because they are the only two humans in the Bible that did not die and Hebrews 9:27 says that "people are destined to die once."

Any of these views are possible, but until that day comes, the identity of these two remains a holy mystery.

QUESTION #10: WHAT ABOUT THE RESURRECTION OF THE DEAD?

The Bible is filled with examples of and discussions about *resurrection*. The apostle Paul argued that the resurrection of Jesus is the central pillar of the Christian faith (see 1 Corinthians 15). An important reminder: resurrection refers only to the raising of one's physical *body*. The clear teaching of scripture is that at death, one's immaterial essence, the soul or spirit, is immediately either with the Lord, enjoying forever bliss, or separated from Him, experiencing eternal woe (see Luke 16:22–23; 2 Corinthians 5:8; Philippians 1:23).

In the Old Testament, we see some resurrections. Both Elijah and Elisha raised people from the dead (1 Kings 17:8–24; 2 Kings 4:18–37; see also 2 Kings 13:21). In the Gospels, Jesus raised Jairus's daughter (Mark 5:35–43), the only son of a widow from Nain (Luke

7:11–16), and His friend Lazarus (John 11). The apostles Peter and Paul raised people from the dead (Acts 9:36–42; 20:9–12).

There were other resurrections. At the death of Christ, Matthew reported, "The bodies of many holy people who had died were raised to life. They came out of the tombs after Jesus' resurrection" (Matthew 27:52–53).

These, however, were only sporadic incidents, signs of something bigger to come. According to Jesus in John 5:28–29 (see also Luke 14:13–14; 1 Corinthians 15:22–23; 1 Thessalonians 4:13–16), there will one day be a wide-scale "resurrection of life" and "resurrection of judgment" (John 5:29 NASB; see also Revelation 20:4–6).

Some—primarily dispensational believers—expect a series of resurrections. They note that when the Lord comes down from heaven, the "dead in Christ will rise first" (1 Thessalonians 4:13–18; see also 1 Corinthians 15:51–58). This resurrection of the "dead in Christ" reunites deceased Christians with their glorified bodies. First Thessalonians 4 also suggests that immediately after this event all living Christians "will be caught . . . to meet the Lord in the air" (verse 17). This is more of a transition into glory rather than a strict resurrection.

Dispensationalists also cite passages such as Revelation 20:4–6 and Daniel 12:2 to suggest that the resurrection of saints who died before the church age began will not take place until the beginning of the millennial reign of Christ. They see the millennium as a time when all believers in Jesus—Jews and Gentiles, those raptured and those resurrected—will share in Christ's kingdom glory (Matthew 8:11). They interpret Revelation 20:5 to mean that the unbelieving dead will be raised at the end of the millennium. Those who follow other interpretational schemes anticipate only a single resurrection at the end of history.

Jesus said that "famines and earthquakes in various places" would be "the beginning of birth pains" related to the tribulation (Matthew 24:7–8).

QUESTION #11: WHAT IS "THE GREAT TRIBULATION"?

The Greek word translated *tribulation* is *thlipsis*, meaning "a pressing or crushing together." In a general sense, *tribulation* means affliction, distress, persecution, or suffering. Sometimes such troubles are the result of unfaithfulness to God (see Deuteronomy 4:30). Often, however, believers suffer because of their faithfulness to God (see John 16:33; Acts 14:22; Revelation 1:9). A recurring theme in the Bible is how God brings glory to Himself by bringing His people through tribulation to salvation.

The Bible also speaks of a specific period of unparalleled tribulation. The prophet Daniel wrote: "There will be a time of distress such as has not happened from the beginning of nations until then. But at that time your people—everyone whose name is found written in the book—will be delivered" (Daniel 12:1). Jesus said, "For then there will be great distress, unequaled from the beginning of the world until now—and never to be equaled again" (Matthew 24:21; see also Mark 13:19).

"Great distress . . . never to be equaled again." No wonder the Bible speaks so often—and at such length—about this event that is variously called "a time of trouble for Jacob" (Jeremiah 30:7), Daniel's seventieth week (Daniel 9:27), and "the hour of trial that is going to come on the whole world" (Revelation 3:10). The prophet Zephaniah gave it this lengthy, ominous description: "That day will be a day of wrath—a day of distress and anguish, a day of trouble and ruin, a day of darkness and gloom, a day of clouds and blackness" (Zephaniah 1:15).

Because of Daniel 9:24–27, Christians who embrace premillennialism expect this future time of tribulation to last seven years. And some think the final three and a half years of this period will feature exponentially more wrath and judgment than the first half of the period. Thus, some refer to the entire seven-year period as "the tribulation" and the final half as "the great tribulation." The Bible suggests multiple purposes for this grim time: to fulfill prophecies made about Israel; to offer the world a final opportunity to turn to God and serve Him (2 Peter 3:9; Revelation 7); to pour out judgment on unrepentant unbelievers (Revelation 6:17).

As pointed out earlier, those who understand these passages in a historical way rather than in a futurist sense see these prophecies as describing what took place in the first century AD.

Natural phenomena can be frightening, but the Bible describes a terrifying "day of the Lord" when God will pour out His wrath against sin over the whole earth.

QUESTION #12: WHAT IS THE "DAY OF THE LORD"?

People sometimes call Sunday, the day Christians routinely gather to worship, the Lord's Day. This is not what is meant by the biblical phrase "day of the Lord" (1 Thessalonians 5:2), or "that day" (Mark 13:32), or "day of vengeance" (Isaiah 61:2; 63:4). Such phrases are a way of referring to a time of cataclysmic judgment at the end of history.

A few prophetic verses that speak of this coming day:

* ✳ "But that day belongs to the Lord, the LORD Almighty—a day of vengeance, for vengeance on his foes" (Jeremiah 46:10).

✳ "The LORD Almighty has a day in store for all the proud and lofty" (Isaiah 2:12).

✳ "Alas for that day! For the day of the LORD is near; it will come like destruction from the Almighty" (Joel 1:15).

✳ "The day of the LORD is near for all nations. As you have done, it will be done to you; your deeds will return upon your own head" (Obadiah 15).

The day will come without warning (1 Thessalonians 5:2; 2 Thessalonians 2:2; 2 Peter 3:10; Revelation 6:17). It will be "dreadful" (Joel 2:31) because in it God will rightly punish those who stubbornly defy Him and spurn His lordship and love. He will judge sin, deliver His people, and triumph over His enemies.

Scholars debate how long this "day" will be—perhaps an actual twenty-four-hour day or a longer period of time. Many equate this day with all or part of the seven-year tribulation period.

QUESTION #13: WHAT DOES *ANTICHRIST* MEAN?

Antichrist, or *antichristos* in Greek, is a term found only in the apostle John's letters (1 John 2:18, 22; 4:3; 2 John 7). Scholars often debate whether *antichrist* is a general term for anyone who opposes God, His people, and His plans or whether it refers more properly to a single end-times individual. This is not an either-or question; it is a both-and proposition. Many have an antichrist spirit, *and* one specific individual will step forward in the last days to oppose God and what He is doing through Jesus. This powerful figure will deceive many and turn them against Jesus.

A number of biblical characters—some who held great power—hinted at the coming Antichrist with their antagonism to the Jewish people, temple, or capital city of Jerusalem:

* The serpent in the Garden of Eden, who attempted to ruin God's good creation (Genesis 3)
* Pharaoh, who enslaved the Hebrews in Egypt (Exodus 1:11, 22; 5:2)
* King Nebuchadnezzar of Babylon, who destroyed the temple in Jerusalem, persecuted Israel in exile, and presumed to possess God-like sovereignty (2 Kings 24:13–14; Daniel 4:30).
* Haman, an enemy of the Jewish people who attempted genocide against them in Persia (the book of Esther)

In opposing Jesus, the Pharisees—shown here asking the Lord whether they should pay taxes to Caesar—were "antichrist." But the Bible describes an evil end-times character that many identify with the term.

Jesus never used the term *antichrist*. He did, however, warn of those who would come claiming to be the Messiah (Matthew 24:5), and He echoed Daniel's prophecy about "the abomination that causes desolation" (Matthew 24:15).

The apostle Paul also did not use the word *antichrist*. Instead, he used the phrase "man of lawlessness" (2 Thessalonians 2:3–4). This character tries to steal worship that belongs only to God (Revelation 13:4–8).

John did not use the word *antichrist* in Revelation; however, his vision included a mysterious figure fiercely antagonistic to God. Could this be an end-times world leader who will combine rare political skill with great spiritual influence? Many read Revelation 13 and say, "Absolutely."

QUESTION #14: WHAT DOES REVELATION MEAN BY THE DRAGON AND THE TWO BEASTS?

Those who read Revelation 12 and 13 are fascinated by mentions of "an enormous red dragon" (12:3) and "a beast coming out of the sea" (13:1) and "a second beast, coming out of the earth" (13:11). What are we to make of these characters?

John described the dragon as having seven heads and ten horns. In Revelation 12:9, he identified the dragon as "that ancient serpent called the devil, or Satan, who leads the whole world astray." He depicted him as trying to devour the male child of a woman about to give birth, which some interpret as Christ.

John also mentioned two "beasts." The first is seen rising out of the sea and bears some of the same characteristics of the four beasts mentioned in Daniel 7: ten horns, seven heads, features resembling a leopard, bear, and lion (Revelation 13:1–2). John wrote, "The dragon gave the beast his power and his throne and great authority" (Revelation 13:2). This beast is described as blasphemous and

"Then war broke out in heaven. Michael and his angels fought against the dragon, and the dragon and his angels fought back" (Revelation 12:7).

vicious against "God's holy people" (Revelation 13:7). Most Bible interpreters identify this beast as the Antichrist.

According to the preterist view, this beast may have been the evil Roman emperor Nero. According to the futurist view, the first beast may end up being a Gentile leader who will effectively rule the world in the end times. They see biblical references to the "little" horn in Daniel 7:8 and the "man doomed to destruction" in 2 Thessalonians 2:3 as applying to this ruler.

Some say that the seven heads and ten horns of the beast in Revelation 17 represent seven past and ten future kings (see verses 10–12). The seven kings may stand for seven political powers that have persecuted Israel throughout history. Others speculate that the ten horns represent the Roman governors involved in the violent civil dispute of AD 68 to 69. Others see the ten horns as suggesting a future federation of governments out of which this figure will arise.

A second beast, said to be "coming out of the earth" (Revelation 13:11) is described as having two horns. John wrote, "It exercised all the authority of the first beast on its behalf, and made the earth and its inhabitants worship the first beast" (Revelation 13:12; see also Revelation 13:14–17). In John's vision this figure acted as a kind of mouthpiece for the first beast and was given the power to perform wonders and miracles, and thereby "deceived the inhabitants of the earth" (Revelation 13:14). Some refer to this beast as "the false prophet" (Revelation 16:13; 19:20).

Together these three evil personages—Satan, the Antichrist, and the false prophet—make up a false and evil trinity, mocking and opposing the holy trinity of God the Father, God the Son, and God the Holy Spirit.

Many believe the Jezreel Valley of northern Israel will be the site of the end-times battle of Armageddon.

QUESTION #15: WHAT DOES THE BIBLE SAY ABOUT ARMAGEDDON?

Armageddon is mentioned once in the Bible, in Revelation 16:16. It's said to be the place where the "kings of the whole world" will gather "for the battle on the great day of God Almighty" (Revelation 16:14). Most prophecy scholars see this as a reference to a great climactic battle between the forces of God and forces of evil in the last days—either literal or spiritual. Literalists question where exactly this battle will take place.

One popular theory is that it will happen at Megiddo, an ancient military stronghold (Joshua 12:21; 17:11; Judges 1:27; 2 Kings 9:27) on the southwest edge of the plain of Esdraelon. A number of biblical battles were fought in or around this area, including ones between Israel and Sisera (Judges 5:19–20) and Josiah and Pharaoh Necho of Egypt (2 Kings 23:29). Regardless of where this final battle will take place, Armageddon points to an ultimate clash between God and the forces of evil.

QUESTION #16: WHAT'S THE MEANING OF *MILLENNIUM*?

When Christians speak of the millennium, they're referring to the millennial reign of Christ. Six times in Revelation 20:2–7, the phrase "thousand years" is used in reference to Satan being bound (verse 2) and Jesus reigning and ruling.

There are at least four different ways Christians understand this phrase and concept:

Postmillennialism is a view that enjoyed more popularity in the nineteenth century, prior to the two great world wars and the increasing evil of the twentieth century. It anticipates the Gospel's power to change lives and culture. It sees a great spiritual revival ushering in a time of unprecedented peace and prosperity on the earth, *after* which Jesus will return to judge the wicked. Those on Jesus' side will enter an eternal new heaven and new earth (Revelation 21:1). Postmillennialists do not see Israel and the church as distinct entities.

Amillennialism is a more popular view. The prefix "a" in amillennialism means "no" or "not." Thus, an amillennialist believes in "no (literal) millennium." He or she interprets the phrase "thousand years" figuratively—that is, it's an allegorical or symbolic way of saying "a long time." In amillennialism, the reign of Christ, the kingdom of God, though real, is spiritual in nature. It's in the hearts of believers right now. Thus, there's no need to look for Jesus to have a physical, thousand-year reign on the earth before the last judgment. He defeated Satan by His perfect life and sacrificial death. He began to reign when He rose from the dead.

An angel binds Satan, throwing him "into the Abyss" for a thousand years (Revelation 20:1–3).

237

He currently sits on the throne of David, and the kingdom over which He rules is the existing church age. Good and evil will continue in the world until He returns, at which time the dead will be raised and judgment will take place. References in the Bible to a future perfect kingdom actually point to a time beyond time, when God will make all things new in "a new heaven and a new earth" (Revelation 21:1).

Historical premillennialism sees Christ returning to earth and immediately establishing His millennial reign. His return is *before* the millennium. In this viewpoint, Christ's reign isn't necessarily a literal thousand years. However, during this time, it is thought that the Old Testament system of worship and sacrifice will be reinstituted (Ezekiel 43:18–46:24). At the end of the millennial reign, Satan will be loosed (Revelation 20:7–8), and Gog and Magog (Ezekiel 38–39) will rise against God's kingdom (and be defeated). After this, the final judgment will occur.

Historical premillennialists don't distinguish between the rapture and the second coming of Christ; they see them as the same event. They do believe that certain events must take place before Jesus can return, such as the appearance of the beast and the false prophet (Revelation 13).

Dispensational premillennialism teaches the idea that Jesus will rapture His church (1 Corinthians 15:51–52; 1 Thessalonians 4:15–17) either prior to or during a seven-year tribulation period on earth (Daniel 9:24–27) at the end of human history. After the tribulation, Jesus will return again, judge the world, bind Satan (Revelation 20:1–3), and establish a literal, thousand-year earthly kingdom. He will rule with His saints from the throne of David (Luke 1:32) in Jerusalem (Isaiah 2:3; Matthew 24:27–31; Revelation 19:11–21). During His reign, the Old Testament system of worship and sacrifice will be reinstituted (Ezekiel 43:18–46:24). The earth will be prosperous and peaceful (Isaiah 2:4; 11:6–9).

At the end of a thousand years, Satan will be released and he will make one final, futile effort to defeat Jesus (Revelation 20:7–9). At the great white throne judgment (Revelation 20:11–15), the devil and all unbelievers will be hurled into "the lake of fire." Believers will live forever in a new heaven and new earth (Revelation 21:1). The dispensational premillennialist maintains that Israel and the church are two separate entities, and that God has a specific redemption plan for each.

Jesus separates the saved from the lost in an etching by Jan Luyken (1649–1712).

THE *BEMA* SEAT

In 2 Corinthians 5:9–11, Paul referred to the "judgment seat of Christ." The Greek word is *bema*. In the first century, this was the name for an elevated platform from which people would give public speeches, where athletes would receive prizes, or where legal charges would be brought against people. Paul described the judgment seat of Christ as an event during which followers of Jesus will receive an evaluation for works done in the body, whether good or bad (Romans 14:10–12; 2 Corinthians 5:9–11).

Whichever view a person believes about the millennium, Christian believers agree on one thing: they can each have Jesus reigning in their hearts and lives right now.

QUESTION #17: THE COMING JUDGMENT

One of the recurring themes of scripture is that God is a just judge who can be trusted to reward or punish each person accordingly (Psalms 28:4; 62:12; Romans 2:6; Revelation 2:23; 18:6; 22:12). This would not be good news were it not for the gospel of Jesus. The Gospel says that Jesus graciously took the punishment of death that we sinners deserved and also offered us all the blessings and rewards He deserved. We access this sounds-too-good-to-be-true offer by putting our trust in Jesus.

In Revelation 20, John reported, "Then I saw a great white throne and him who was seated on it." In John's vision, "the dead, great and small," stood before the throne while "books were opened," and were "judged according to what they had done" as recorded in the books. One of the books John saw opened was "the book of life" (verses 11–15).

Known as the great white throne judgment, this is regarded as the final, sobering event before the beginning of the eternal "new heaven and a new earth" (Revelation 21:1).

Some Christians (amillennialists and postmillennialists) believe this to be the final judgment of all people—believers and unbelievers. Ultimately, what matters is whether a person's name is included in the book of life. Many premillennialists insist this is a judgment of unbelievers only—that Christians will be exempt from this judgment because their sins were judged and forgiven in Christ's death, and because their works will have been judged at the judgment seat of Christ (2 Corinthians 5:10) sometime after the rapture.

The chapter ends with this warning: "Anyone whose name was not found written in the book of life was thrown into the lake of fire" (Revelation 20:15).

QUESTION #18: WHAT ABOUT HELL?

We just looked at Revelation 20, which speaks of a "lake of fire" (verses 14–15) or "lake of burning sulfur" (verse 10). The Bible

To some observers, recent California wildfires are reminiscent of the Bible's descriptions of hell.

describes this as a place where the devil, the beast, the false prophet, and ultimately *all* the wicked will end up "tormented day and night for ever and ever" (Revelation 20:10). Throughout the Bible, fire is often linked to punishment and destruction. Many times it is also associated with brimstone or sulfur, such as in the judgment of Sodom and Gomorrah (Genesis 19:24; see also Revelation 14:10–11).

Is the lake of fire a description of hell? The Bible uses four different terms to speak of the destination of the dead: Sheol, Hades, Gehenna, and Tartarus.

The Old Testament Hebrew word is *sheol*. It refers broadly to the abode of all the dead, without distinguishing between the righteous and unrighteous dead. Various English translations of the Bible render the word *sheol* as "pit," "grave," "death," or "destruction." It's described as a place of silence (Psalm 94:17) and "utter darkness" (Job 10:21).

In the New Testament at least three Greek words are used to speak of hell. *Hades* is a synonym of the Hebrew word *sheol*. It refers simply to the realm of the dead. Hades and Sheol are not the same as what we think of as hell—that is, a permanent place of punishment. Rather, they seem to describe a temporary holding place where souls await final judgment to either heaven or hell.

The word *Gehenna* is actually derived from a name: the Valley of Ben Hinnom, south of Jerusalem. It was in this ravine that the Jewish people engaged in the heinous practice of child sacrifice (2 Chronicles 28:3; 33:6). By the time of Christ, Hinnom, or Gehenna, was essentially a garbage dump, a place of defilement where the bodies of executed criminals were tossed, and where refuse and rubbish were continually burned. Gehenna was a smoldering, terrible place. Thus, when Jesus talked about hell being a place "where the fire never goes out" (Mark 9:43), His audience had a powerful image to help them grasp His meaning.

The apostle Peter used another term from Greek mythology to speak of hell: the word *Tartarus* (2 Peter 2:4). This term isn't found anywhere else in the Bible. It means to "cast into hell." Peter's point in this verse is that this is what happened to the angels who sinned. They are being "held for judgment" in "chains of darkness."

Scripture describes hell as a place of utter darkness (Matthew 22:13) and restless torment (Revelation 14:10–11). It's a place where unrepentant unbelievers experience separation from God for eternity (2 Thessalonians 1:9).

The good news is that the apostle John explained how a person can be sure that their eternal destiny is with God, not separated from Him: "And this is the testimony: God has given us eternal life, and this life is in his Son. Whoever has the Son has life; whoever does not have the Son of God does not have life. I write these things to you who believe in the name of the Son of God so that you may know that you have eternal life" (1 John 5:11–13).

A nuclear weapons test in 1946. Many have speculated that atomic weapons will bring about the end of the world, an interpretation that some say 2 Peter 3:7 supports. *See Question #19 on next page.*

QUESTION #19: DOES "THE END OF THE WORLD" MEAN THE END OF THE WORLD?

In 2 Peter 3:7, we read that "the present heavens and earth are reserved for fire, being kept for the day of judgment and destruction of the ungodly" (2 Peter 3:7).

Those who interpret this literally believe that during the great judgment at the end of the tribulation, God will send fire to destroy the heavens and the earth as we know it. Dispensational premillennialists point to verses such as 1 Thessalonians 1:10 and 5:9 to suggest that believers will not be present on earth when this happens. They see this catastrophic event as a "starting over" before the beginning of the millennium.

QUESTION #20: WHAT DOES THE BIBLE MEAN BY "A NEW HEAVEN AND A NEW EARTH"?

Many people think of eternity as a kind of endless, ghostly, ethereal existence—spirits floating around in the clouds, playing harps for ever and ever. That's not the picture of heaven we see in the Bible.

The biblical prophets spoke of a glorious future day when the broken, marred world we know will be renewed. God will create "a new heaven and a new earth," a new universe free from the curse of sin (Isaiah 65:17–20; Revelation 21–22). We'll have new, resurrected

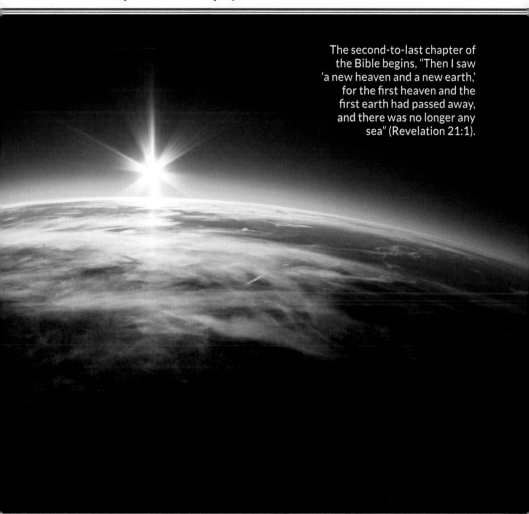

The second-to-last chapter of the Bible begins, "Then I saw 'a new heaven and a new earth,' for the first heaven and the first earth had passed away, and there was no longer any sea" (Revelation 21:1).

THE MARRIAGE SUPPER OF THE LAMB

In Revelation 19:9, an angel told John to write, "Blessed are those who are invited to the wedding supper of the Lamb!" This end-times imagery conforms to the wedding customs of the ancient Near East. A procession to the bride's home would be followed by an elaborate and joyous wedding banquet. This is a metaphorical picture of Christ's triumphal procession from heaven to earth to receive His bride—the church. This event is foreshadowed in the Old Testament (Isaiah 25:6) and is a beautiful, prophetic picture of what awaits the people of God. Imagine being invited to a lavish party where God is the host—that's what Christ has made possible for those who put their faith in Him.

bodies that will never tire or get sick, and we will enjoy the benefits of being redeemed and restored, physically and spiritually.

Here are some descriptions of this eternal state in the Bible:

✳ Chaos and evil, which some scholars believe are symbolized by the restless sea, will be history (Revelation 21:1).
✳ There will be no more death or crying or pain (Revelation 21:4).
✳ It will be daylight all the time; there will be no need for the sun or the moon because the glory of the Lord will illuminate all things (Revelation 22:5).
✳ We will live as citizens in the new, beautiful heavenly Jerusalem (Galatians 4:26; Philippians 3:20; Hebrews 12:22;
✳ Revelation 21:2), where the Lord God and the Lamb will live (Revelation 21:22).
✳ We will be able to see God face to face (Revelation 22:4).

Contrary to popular misconceptions about eternal life, it will be anything but boring. According to the apostle John's peek into the future, life in the hereafter will feature brilliant colors (Revelation 21:19–21), abundant food (19:7–9; 22:2), joyful music (5:8–13), and intimate fellowship with God (22:3–4). Above all, there will be unending adoration of Jesus and praise and service to Him.

We've asked and answered twenty questions about things to come. They prompt one more question that every person should personally answer: What can possibly compare to the breathtaking beauty and satisfaction of life with God, both here and now and forevermore in the new heaven and the new earth?

Conclusion:

WHILE WE WAIT . . .

Chapter 10:

HERE'S WHAT WE CAN SAY FOR SURE

J. Barton Payne, in his massive *Encyclopedia of Biblical Prophecy*, lists a total of 1,817 Bible prophecies—1,239 from the Old Testament and 578 from the New Testament. By his count, these ancient predictions make up 8,352 verses of scripture, or slightly more than a fourth of the Bible. Even the scholars who don't universally agree with Payne's totals agree that prophecy is a central and significant aspect of scripture.

Hundreds of these prophecies have been fulfilled in history. Some of them seem fairly broad, so it's understandable when a person says, "That seems vague to me." But many other prophecies are incredibly specific, foretelling even a person's name (Isaiah 44:28; 45:1).

So we're left with this question: Could all this Bible prophecy be pure chance, a string of lucky guesses, sort of like winning the lottery? Or put another way, what are the odds that all these fulfilled prophecies are just giant coincidences?

Not good. In fact, infinitesimal.

Take just eleven of the many Old Testament predictions about the Messiah. According to these, He would be

* born to a certain tribe and family (Isaiah 11:1–2)
* born in a certain town (Micah 5:2–5)
* almost killed in infancy (Jeremiah 31:15)
* exiled briefly in Egypt (Hosea 11:1)
* betrayed for thirty pieces of silver (Zechariah 11:12–13)
* struck on the head with a rod (Micah 5:1)
* stripped naked, with others casting lots for His clothing (Psalm 22:18)
* pierced in His hands and feet (Psalm 22:16)
* buried with the rich (Isaiah 53:9)
* raised from the dead (Psalm 16:8–11)

How many of these details could a person arrange in advance? Granted, someone could read various Old Testament passages about the Messiah and set out to fulfill *some* of them. But not these—not when they involve the actions of others.

In 1958, Peter W. Stoner and Robert C. Newman wrote a book titled *Science Speaks.* The authors calculated the probability of any one man fulfilling just eight out of sixty major Old Testament prophecies about the Messiah. They suggested the likelihood of this was one in ten to the seventeenth power, which comes to roughly one in one hundred quadrillion.

Whether or not Stoner and Newman's math is correct (and whether such things can even be calculated with precision), one thing is clear: The fulfillment of so many prophecies in the life of Jesus

Mary Magdalene falls at the feet of Jesus, recently arisen from the dead. The resurrection was one of numerous aspects of Jesus' life addressed by the prophets.

was—and is—no accident. In fact, it strongly suggests two things: (1) The Bible is the trustworthy Word of God, not any old book; and (2) Jesus is the Christ, the Savior of the world.

In the first part of this book, we looked at some of the hundreds of Bible prophecies that have been fulfilled. Many of them, such as those cited above, are messianic in nature and have been perfectly fulfilled in the life of Jesus. In part two, we examined a number of biblical predictions that many Christians claim are yet to be fulfilled.

In our investigation, we've seen that Christians interpret Bible prophecies in a variety of ways. Some take a more literal approach, whereas others understand these ancient predictions in a more figurative or spiritualized way. But even with different views about how to understand end-times prophecies, and despite many contested points of eschatology, there are still a few biblical truths that all followers of Jesus can agree on and cling to.

Here are three truths beyond debate when we're engaging with tricky, complicated, and sometimes confusing eschatology:

1. God is in control.
2. Jesus is coming again.
3. Christians are called to watch, hope, and shine.

In this final chapter, let's look briefly at each of those truths.

1. GOD IS IN CONTROL.

From beginning to end, the Bible says that God is sovereign over the universe. He's the creator, sustainer, and orchestrator of life. As we sing in the Christmas song, He rules the world "with truth and grace." We can't always see that He's reigning; the world seems awfully chaotic at times. Yet *nothing* happens outside of His sovereign will.

God's sovereignty doesn't make Him the author of evil; on the contrary, it means that, despite the freedom or agency that humans have been given, God has the power to overcome evil with good—and even to bring good out of evil (Genesis 50:20). Consider just a few biblical statements along those lines:

* ✳ "The LORD does whatever pleases him, in the heavens and on the earth" (Psalm 135:6; see also Psalm 115:3).
* ✳ "Many are the plans in a person's heart, but it is the LORD's purpose that prevails" (Proverbs 19:21).

* "The king's heart is a stream of water in the hand of the LORD; he turns it wherever he will" (Proverbs 21:1 ESV).

* "I make known the end from the beginning, from ancient times, what is still to come. I say, 'My purpose will stand, and I will do all that I please'" (Isaiah 46:10).

* The humbled Nebuchadnezzar said, "[God] does as he pleases with the powers of heaven and the peoples of the earth. No one can hold back his hand or say to him: 'What have you done?'" (Daniel 4:35).

* "And we know that in all things God works for the good of those who love him, who have been called according to his purpose" (Romans 8:28).

The truth of God's sovereignty is vital to us. Why? Because without it, many of the things we see happening around us, and many of the things prophesied in the book of Revelation, would lead us to believe that the world is spinning out of control and headed toward hopelessness.

It is not. God is involved in the affairs of humanity. He's at work, even in the hearts of unlikely people and even in the midst of terrible situations. The words of the famed nineteenth-century pastor Charles Spurgeon are helpful here: "God is too good to be unkind and He is too wise to be mistaken. And when we cannot trace His hand, we must trust His heart."

God speaks to Job from a whirlwind in an early nineteenth-century painting by William Blake. Job suffered tragic losses at the hand of Satan, but only what God allowed.

GOD IS IN THE DETAILS.

In Jeremiah 29, we read a remarkable letter that the prophet wrote to the Jewish exiles in Babylon. In it, he encouraged the people to "settle down" into their new place and to "seek the peace and prosperity" of Babylon, where God had brought them (verses 5, 7). In other words, *You're not going anywhere anytime soon. You'll come home only after the seventy years God prophesied for you to spend in exile are over.*

Jeremiah went on to write a verse so many Christians love: "'For I know the plans I have for you,' declares the LORD" (verse 11).

One point of this passage is that we serve a God of details. He's always with His people, orchestrating, watching, planning, providing. We can trust God with the big picture as well as with the finest brushstrokes of our lives.

A second non-debatable truth—at least to anyone who has read the Bible—is that Jesus is coming again.

2. JESUS IS COMING AGAIN.

The return of Christ is the great climax to the biblical story. It's what every believer lives for and hopes for. Exactly *when* Christ will come is a topic open for discussion. As we've seen, people have all sorts of ideas and theories and interpretations. But other than those who hold a strict preterist view, no orthodox, mainstream Christian denies the fundamental promise that Christ *will* return to earth in glory one day.

The second coming of Jesus is one of the most prophesied events in the Bible. The prophet Isaiah spoke of a day when the Messiah will "slay the wicked" (Isaiah 11:4), "reign on Mount Zion and in Jerusalem" (Isaiah 24:23), and rule "on David's throne and over his kingdom,

In His first coming, Jesus arrived on earth as a baby. In His second coming, He will be the all-powerful King.

establishing and upholding it with justice and righteousness from that time on and forever" (Isaiah 9:7).

David said in Psalm 22:27–31 that the Messiah would one day be given dominion over the entire earth. In Psalm 47, the sons of Korah rejoiced over the coming day when the Lord would be "the great King over all the earth" (verse 2). Seeing this future event as though it had already happened, the author wrote about how the Lord "subdued nations" (verse 3).

The prophets Jeremiah, Ezekiel, and Daniel all predicted that the Lord would one day gather dispersed Jews from the ends of the earth and bring them back to the land of Israel (Jeremiah 33:6–18;

see Ezekiel 20:33-44; Daniel 7:13-14, 18, 27). The claim that the Messiah would return and be glorified before His saints and all the peoples of the earth is a recurring Old Testament prophetic theme (see Psalm 46:10; Isaiah 52:10, 13).

In the New Testament, it's more of the same. Jesus talked explicitly about returning in glory (Matthew 25). And when He ascended into heaven, angels told His gawking followers, "Men of Galilee . . . why do you stand here looking into the sky? This same Jesus, who has been taken from you into heaven, will come back in the same way you have seen him go into heaven" (Acts 1:11).

In his first letter to the Thessalonians, Paul comforted this fledgling church by reminding them that Jesus will return in glory (4:16-18).

A person may legitimately say, "I don't believe that Jesus will come back to earth." But no person who's ever read the Bible can allege, "The Christian faith doesn't teach that Jesus will come again."

A final truth regarding the end times, something all believers can agree on, is that Christians are called to live as salt and light as they watch hopefully for Christ's return.

FROM BAD TO WORSE

The Bible makes it clear that in earth's last days we will see an increase in worldly-minded "mockers." These are people who follow their own desires, reject the truth of God, deny the possibility of the second coming of Christ, and scoff at the idea of coming judgment (2 Peter 3:3-4). You probably know people like this. According to the Bible, cynics and skeptics will always exist, and they will mock anyone who believes. Spiritual leaders, however, follow Paul's admonition in Titus 1:9 to "hold firmly to the trustworthy message as it has been taught" so they might "encourage others by sound doctrine and refute those who oppose it."

3. CHRISTIANS ARE CALLED TO WATCH, HOPE, AND SHINE.

Even though no one can state with certainty when the Lord will return, there's much we can do before that day arrives. True believers are not in darkness (1 Thessalonians 5:4–5). Jesus and the apostles left clear instructions to show us how to prepare.

Jesus told His followers to watch for signals that His return was imminent. He warned of "wars and rumors of wars" (Matthew 24:6), famines, earthquakes, a rise in persecution of believers, and an increase in the number of self-proclaimed messiahs and false prophets. "The love of most will grow cold," He prophesied (Matthew 24:12). The approach of such signs shouldn't frighten us but rather call us to action.

In light of such realities, how should we live? What specific things can we do while we look forward to Christ's coming? Here are a few New Testament commands:

Wake up! Spiritual drowsiness is a real condition that affects—or we might say *infects*—a lot of believers. It's why the apostle Paul urged Roman Christians, "The hour has already come for you to wake up from your slumber, because our salvation is nearer now than when we first believed" (Romans 13:11). It was this kind of "narcolepsy of the soul" that prompted Paul to warn the believers in

Individual Christians, churches, and parachurch organizations await Jesus' return by doing good in their communities.

Thessalonica, "We do not belong to the night or to the darkness. So then, let us not be like others, who are asleep, but let us be awake and sober" (1 Thessalonians 5:5–6; see also Ephesians 5:14).

Paul was referring not to physical sleep but to a kind of spiritual slumber or unconsciousness. In biblical times, sleep was a metaphor for dullness or shirking one's responsibility (Proverbs 6:4–10). The Bible says many, even in the church, will be deceived before the return of Jesus, so Christians are called to be spiritually alert.

Be on the lookout! Being awake serves no good purpose unless one is also keeping watch. "Watching" is a prominent theme in the Bible (Psalm 130:6; Isaiah 62:6; Jeremiah 31:6). A watchman is vigilant, wary, and protective. His role is to stay awake and to warn others of looming trouble. Watchfulness is also a mark of those who follow Jesus. As He told His disciples, "Be on guard! Be alert!" (Mark 13:33, see also Romans 13:11–14).

Pray! Concerning the end times, Jesus said, "Be always on the watch, *and pray*" (Luke 21:36, emphasis added). In other words, don't stop at being vigilant and watchful—also lift your eyes and your concerns to heaven. Ask God to open hearts. Then ask God to open your heart and mind and fill you with His truth, so that you can be His instrument and servant.

"Be always on the watch, and pray that you may be able to escape all that is about to happen, and that you may be able to stand before the Son of Man" (Luke 21:36).

Be comfortable with mystery. The infinite God has given finite humans His eternal Word. He calls us to study it diligently (2 Timothy 2:15). We should do so with faith, trusting He will show us all the things about Bible prophecy He wants us to know. However, we also need to remember that in the sovereign wisdom of God, He has chosen *not* to reveal certain details regarding the end times (Acts 1:7). With regard to some questions, there is no shame—in fact there is great humility and wisdom—in saying, "I don't know." One day, we will see everything clearly (1 Corinthians 13:12).

WHAT DOES IT MEAN TO BE DISCERNING?

When people were advocating all sorts of weird and wrong ideas, Isaiah's advice was, "Consult God's instruction and the testimony of warning. If anyone does not speak according to this word, they have no light of dawn" (Isaiah 8:20). *That* is what it means to be discerning. It's learning how to separate truth from error. Discernment is a trait that is desperately needed in our dark times. While some of the ideas that people spout are simply goofy and misguided, others are flat-out wrong and evil. Realize that we live in an era in which anyone can declare himself or herself a pastor or spiritual leader or guru, start a podcast, and immediately start spreading cockamamie ideas to a vast audience. And many are doing precisely this.

Discerning Christians realize that the Bible is their plumb line, their absolute authority. They measure everything they hear against it. Before you accept ideas in a streamed message, before you swallow hook, line and sinker some teaching posted on a blog, check these things closely against the Word of God (Acts 17:11). The best way to guard against being tricked by the evil one is by having a robust understanding of God's Word.

Remain hopeful. We often use the word *hope* when what we really mean is *wish*. For example, the kid who says wistfully—with fingers crossed—"I hope I get a go-cart for Christmas." This is a far cry from biblical hope. When Paul told the Roman believers, "Be joyful in hope" (Romans 12:12), he wasn't telling believers to grab their lucky rabbit's foot. He was talking about *a confident expectation* that Jesus *is* coming back and that all will be well in the end. In fact, at the conclusion of this same letter, Paul wrote, "I pray that God, the source of hope, will fill you completely with joy and peace because you trust in him. Then you will overflow with confident hope through the power of the Holy Spirit" (Romans 15:13 NLT).

Stand firm. Paul exhorted the believers in Corinth, "Therefore, my dear brothers and sisters, stand firm. Let nothing move you" (1 Corinthians 15:58). The idea in the phrase "stand firm" is to be settled, fixed, immovable. In Ephesians 6:10–13, Paul begged believers, "Take your stand against the devil's schemes." A person who lives in this way is steady. He or she doesn't blow to and fro with the winds of culture. The masses might call this being stubborn or rigid, but God calls it *being faithful.*

A French church window depicts the bishop of Bayeaux resisting the devil, as James 4:7 commands.

THE UNWELCOME PROMISE

For the most part, North American culture has accommodated, or at least tolerated, Christians and Christianity. Because of this, it's easy to forget that the Lord was *killed* for advocating the same ideas we claim to embrace and champion. On His last night with His disciples, Jesus made this grim promise: "If the world hates you, keep in mind that it hated me first. If you belonged to the world, it would love you as its own. As it is, you do not belong to the world, but I have chosen you out of the world. That is why the world hates you. . . . If they persecuted me, they will persecute you also" (John 15:18–20).

This promise/prophecy began being fulfilled soon after Jesus' death. James was martyred by King Herod. Tradition says all the other apostles, except for John, died for the sake of the Gospel. Twenty centuries later, Christians in many parts of the world have to worship in secret. Some watch their pastors suffer torture and imprisonment.

And yet, there is hope amid the horror. God can and does use suffering for His glory and for the spread of the Gospel. And He promises that He will never leave or forsake His children. As persecution increases in our day, believers need to pray for their brothers and sisters who are suffering. Amazingly, they don't ask to be spared *from* persecution; they ask to be faithful in and through it. They want to show and tell the truth of the Gospel.

Be salt and light. Jesus told His first followers, "You are the salt of the earth. . . . You are the light of the world" (Matthew 5:13–14). It is the great privilege and responsibility of believers to live in such a way that they make the people around them thirsty for God's truth and that they shine in the darkness. We can't forget the words written by the apostle Peter to first-century believers: "Always be prepared to give an answer to everyone who asks you to give the reason for the hope that you have" (1 Peter 3:15).

Love well. We live in an era in which it is easy to go online and rant against all the people who don't share our spiritual beliefs. This might make us feel powerful, but it makes God sad. It only gives Christ and His church a black eye. No wonder Paul emphasized the absolute

SPECULATION, PREOCCUPATION, OR PREPARATION?

When it comes to Bible prophecy, we can embrace one of three approaches:

1. We can get caught up in endless speculation about when Jesus will return, about whether this person or that might be the Antichrist, and so on. The truth is that the Son of Man will return when we are not expecting it. It is *not* our responsibility to try to figure out every mystery and detail.

2. We can become complacent and preoccupied with worldly things. Jesus warned, "Be careful, or your hearts will be weighed down with carousing, drunkenness and the anxieties of life, and that day will close on you suddenly like a trap" (Luke 21:34).

3. We can engage in wise preparation. We can ready our hearts and have important spiritual conversations with friends and neighbors. Whether He returns first or whether we die first, we will all meet Jesus soon. Don't you want to meet Him with a pure heart?

The wise believer will live this day with that day in view. He or she will live as though Jesus could show up at any moment. Because in truth, He could.

IS THERE A SPIRITUAL GIFT OF PROPHECY?

In Ephesians 4, Paul listed five types of ministry in the church, one of which is that of a prophet. Some believe that these forms of service were only for the early church and ended when the New Testament was complete. Others believe they still exist within local church bodies.

Separate from, but closely related to, the five ministries are the seven gifts of the Holy Spirit, one of which is the gift of prophecy (Romans 12:6). Some think this means a person could have the *gift* of prophecy without actually holding the formal *office* of prophet.

As we would expect, there is much debate about how to think about prophecy in the church today. Some believe that once the inspired biblical books were written, recognized, and collected, prophetic activity was no longer necessary. Others define the gift of prophecy as forthtelling—that is, communicating what the Bible says in a powerful, challenging way. Others believe that God still speaks directly to and through people to communicate specific messages. Any such "words from the Lord" must always corroborate, and never conflict with, God's written Word.

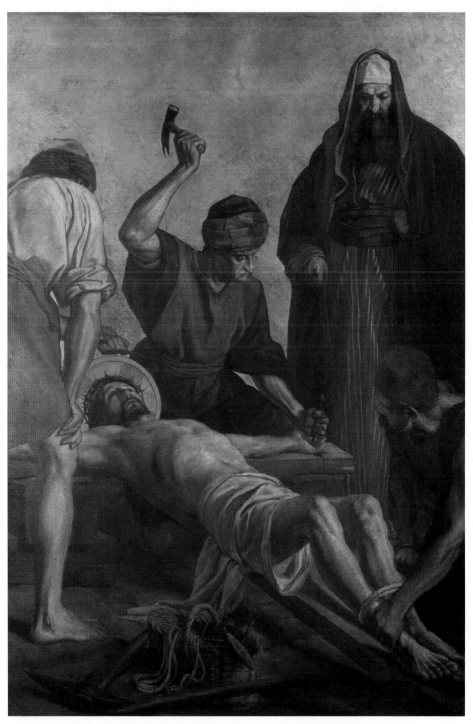

Jesus set a high standard by asking His Father to forgive those who put Him on the cross. We can only follow His example in the power He provides.

necessity of love. He told the Corinthian believers, "If I have the gift of prophecy and can fathom all mysteries and all knowledge, and if I have a faith that can move mountains, but do not have love, I am nothing" (1 Corinthians 13:2). The goal in studying biblical prophecy isn't to have all the answers or to run around setting people straight. Although we want to stand firmly on God's truth, we also want to model His grace (John 1:14, 17). The goal is to love as Christ did, which means loving our enemies, the very ones who mock and mistreat us. He called us to be ambassadors of good news, not judges of ungodly people. Let's leave all the judgment up to Him.

Expect a reward. Scripture indicates that believers who faithfully endure will receive great blessing. To the church at Smyrna, Jesus promised, "Be faithful, even to the point of death, and I will give you life as your victor's crown" (Revelation 2:10). To the church at Philadelphia (in what is modern-day Turkey), Jesus said, "I am coming soon. Hold on to what you have, so that no one will take your crown" (Revelation 3:11).

Chicago pastor Erwin Lutzer once told a story about a farmer who had a loyal dog. The two were inseparable; their love for each other was obvious to all. When the old man died, his body was placed in a coffin, and the coffin was loaded on a train and taken away. From that day forward every time the train pulled into the station, the dog came running, hoping to see his master step out onto the platform.

This is the kind of anticipation God's children should have today and every day. The prophecies already fulfilled in scripture about the first coming of Christ are more than enough to convince us that He is coming again.

Appendix:
PROFILES OF THE PROPHETS

Aaron. The brother of Moses was actually Israel's first high priest. But God told Moses, "Your brother Aaron will be your *prophet*" (Exodus 7:1, emphasis added). Aaron indeed served as Moses' mouthpiece.

Abraham. God told Abimelek, king of Gerar, that the great patriarch of the Jewish people was a prophet (Genesis 20:7).

Agabus. Luke describes Agabus as a prophet from Judea. Agabus predicted a severe famine (see Acts 11:27–28), which ancient historians Josephus, Suetonius, and Tacitus all confirmed. Agabus also correctly prophesied that Paul would be apprehended by the Jews in Jerusalem and turned over to the Gentile authorities (Acts 21:10–11).

Ahijah. A prophet from Shiloh during the time of Solomon, Ahijah tore his robe into twelve pieces and gave Jeroboam ten of the strips to indicate that God would split the nation into a northern kingdom comprising ten tribes, and a southern kingdom made up of the remaining two (1 Kings 11:29–39).

Amos. A contemporary of Old Testament prophets Hosea and Isaiah, Amos directed his blunt prophecies at the northern kingdom of Israel. He was a shepherd and gardener from Tekoa, a town in the southern kingdom of Judah some five miles south of Bethlehem. Amos's ministry occurred during the first half of the eighth century BC when King Jeroboam II's reign was waning (793–753 BC). He decried injustice in an era when the nation was politically strong but spiritually weak.

Anna. Luke described Anna as a prophet from the family of Penuel and the tribe of Asher (Luke 2:36–38). As an elderly woman, she was privileged to be at the temple the day Joseph and Mary brought Jesus to be dedicated. She recognized the infant as the One who would bring about "the redemption of Jerusalem."

Asaph. A Levite musician at the tabernacle, Asaph was appointed along with others "to extol, thank, and praise the Lord, the God of Israel" (1 Chronicles 16:4). He also prophesied under the supervision of King David (see 1 Chronicles 25:1–2).

Azariah. This particular Azariah—there are multiple men in the Bible with this name—was the son of Oded. He called on King Asa to institute some much-needed reforms in Judah (2 Chronicles 15:1–15).

Barnabas. This Cyprian Jew was a leader in the early church. His real name was Joseph, but he earned the nickname Barnabas because he was so encouraging to others. He was a traveling companion of the apostle Paul. In Acts 13:1, he is listed by Luke as part of a group of "prophets and teachers."

Daniel. Daniel was from a royal family and one of the "young . . . handsome . . . well informed, quick to understand" Hebrew youths taken into Babylonian exile (Daniel 1:4). There he served in the royal court, demonstrating remarkable integrity, wisdom, and humility. His visions and dreams are among the most studied passages in the Bible because of what they reveal about the future.

The Daughters of Philip the Evangelist. A Hellenistic Jew, Philip was one of seven men chosen by the early church apostles to supervise the feeding of widows. He had four unmarried daughters whom Luke described as prophets (Acts 21:8–9).

David. We think of David primarily as Israel's greatest king, but many of David's psalms are considered messianic prophecies.

Deborah. The wife of Lappidoth, Deborah was one of Israel's judges and also described as a prophet (Judges 4–5).

Elijah. Perhaps the most famous of the "speaking prophets"—that is, those who didn't leave behind any writings—Elijah ministered in the ninth century BC during the reigns of Ahab and Ahaziah (see 1 Kings 17–2 Kings 2). At that time, Baal worship was beginning to take hold in Israel thanks to Ahab's wife, Jezebel. Elijah never died. He passed on his prophetic mantle to Elisha and was taken up to heaven in a whirlwind (2 Kings 2:11).

Elisha. Elijah's successor, Elisha was the son of Shaphat (1 Kings 19:16). He ministered for about fifty years in the ninth century BC and saw God do extraordinary miracles through his life.

Enoch. The short New Testament letter of Jude speaks of a prophet named Enoch (Jude 1:14). No doubt this is the godly Enoch, the father of Methuselah, who, like Elijah, was transported to heaven without dying (see Genesis 5:18–24).

Ezekiel. From the priestly family of Buzi (Ezekiel 1:3), Ezekiel prophesied during the Babylonian captivity. When his wife died during the exile, he was told by God not to express sorrow (Ezekiel 24:16–18). Through this and other odd signs, Ezekiel sought to call the nation to repentance and also to give them comfort regarding their future.

Gad. Gad prophesied from the final years of Saul's reign through David's reign (1010–970 BC). He advised David to leave Moab and return to Judah (1 Samuel 22:5), and he brought the word of the Lord to David after David sinfully conducted a census of the fighting men of Israel (2 Samuel 24:11–25).

Habakkuk. All we know about Habakkuk comes from the book that bears his name. He lived during the rise of the Babylonian Empire and ministered somewhere between 612 and 589 BC. His message? He wondered why God allowed evil among His people and why God would use a nation even more evil (the Babylonians) to bring judgment on Judah.

Haggai. Little is known about Haggai beyond his four months of ministry around 520 BC, as described in the book that bears his name. He is mentioned in Ezra 5:1 and 6:14, and it was his message that jarred the postexilic community of Jews living in Jerusalem from their spiritual lethargy. Haggai called his fellow citizens to repent and to finish rebuilding the temple.

Hanani. Hanani was a seer who confronted King Asa of Judah for paying the Aramean king Ben-Hadad to attack Israel (2 Chronicles 16:1–10). Because of his boldness, he was imprisoned.

Hosea. We don't know much about this man's life except for what we read in chapters 1 and 3 of the book of Hosea. The son of Beeri, he was commissioned by God to serve as a prophet to Israel during the eight century BC, a time of spiritual and moral decadence. As a painful and humiliating object lesson, the prophet was commanded to marry an immoral woman named Gomer and to remain faithful to her despite her infidelities. His obedience served as a stunning picture of God's love and devotion for His wayward people.

Huldah. This wife of Shallum—an official in King Josiah's court—was recognized as a prophet (2 Kings 22:14). She predicted mercy for the humble Josiah and doom for the nation of Judah after his death (2 Kings 22:15–20).

Iddo. A prophet, or "seer," during Solomon's reign, Iddo is described as having had visions "concerning Jeroboam son of Nebat" (2 Chronicles 9:29). He also recorded information about the reigns of Rehoboam (2 Chronicles 12:15) and Abijah (2 Chronicles 13:22).

Isaiah. A prophet during the eighth century BC, Isaiah's ministry spanned the reigns of four kings of Judah—Uzziah, Jotham, Ahaz, and Hezekiah (Isaiah 1:1). With his wife, also a prophet (see Isaiah 8:3), Isaiah had at least two sons (Isaiah 7:3; 8:3). Isaiah preached against hypocrisy, warned of coming judgment, and wrote extensively about a coming servant  of the Lord. Some have said that his book of sixty-six chapters is like a Bible in miniature: thirty-nine chapters of sin and condemnation, followed by twenty-seven chapters about salvation and restoration.

Jehu. This son of Hanani was the seer who rebuked King Baasha for emulating the pagan ways of Jeroboam (1 Kings 16:1–7). Jehu apparently wrote some things down that have not been preserved for us (2 Chronicles 20:34).

Jeremiah. Known as the "weeping prophet," Jeremiah was the son of Hilkiah from Anathoth (Jeremiah 1:1). He prophesied to the southern kingdom of Judah until it fell to the Babylonians in 586 BC. He is credited with authoring the books of Jeremiah and Lamentations. Because of his strong denunciations of sin and his predictions of Jerusalem's eventual  destruction, the priests and false prophets of Judah labeled Jeremiah a traitor. He suffered beatings, mockery, and imprisonment.

 **Joel.** We know almost nothing about Joel, except that his common name means "The Lord is God." His historical time frame and audience are unclear. All we have are his blunt words about a devastating attack of locusts. This invasion, he said, was symbolic of greater destruction to come on the day of the Lord.

John the Apostle. As an elderly man, the apostle John was exiled to the island of Patmos near the end of the first century. While there, he was given a complex prophetic vision of Jesus, which we know as the book of Revelation.

John the Baptist. John was the son of the aged priest Zechariah and his wife, Elizabeth—who was a relative of Mary, the mother of Jesus (Luke 1:36). He was the forerunner of the Messiah. He lived in the wilderness south of Judea. By roughly AD 27 he was calling the people of Israel to turn back to God and to "make straight the way for the Lord" (John 1:23). John identified Jesus as the "Lamb of God, who takes away the sin of the world!" (John 1:29). He was beheaded by Herod (Matthew 14:10) after he spoke out against Herod's adulterous relationship with Herodias.

Jonah. The son of Amittai (Jonah 1:1), Jonah was a prophet in the northern kingdom of Israel during the first half of the eighth century BC. He followed Elijah and Elisha and preceded Hosea and Amos. Jonah is famous for defying God's command to preach to the people of Nineveh. After a "time-out" inside the belly of a great fish, Jonah reluctantly complied and the Ninevites repented. His story demonstrates God's love for the whole world and His patience with stubborn servants. Some say the Jonah story is only a parable; however, Jesus seemed to view the Jonah story as history (Matthew 12:40–41; Luke 11:29–32).

Lucius of Cyrene. He is mentioned in Luke's list of prophets and teachers from Antioch (Acts 13:1). It's possible he was one of the leaders who preached to the Gentiles when persecution broke out in Jerusalem (Acts 11:19–21).

Malachi. Some have speculated that Malachi's name, which means "my messenger," may have been a title rather than a name. But the writer of the book of Malachi lived in the late fifth century BC. A contemporary of Ezra and Nehemiah, he called the Jews who had returned from Babylonian exile to return also to God.

Manaen. This man, described as a childhood companion of Herod, is mentioned in a list of prophets and teachers in Antioch (Acts 13:1).

Micah. Micah is another of the minor prophets about whom we know very little. Jeremiah mentioned a Micah of Moresheth, who was a prophet during King Hezekiah's reign (Jeremiah 26:17–19). When Micah prophesied doom for Jerusalem, Hezekiah repented, saving Jerusalem from the destruction. Known as the prophet of the poor, Micah was a contemporary of Isaiah.

Micaiah. The son of Imlah, Micaiah was summoned by King Ahab to prophesy doom against the enemy Arameans. Initially, the prophet mockingly told the king exactly what he wanted to hear. When he later told the truth, Ahab tossed him into prison (1 Kings 22:8; 2 Chronicles 18:7–26).

Miriam. This sister of Moses is called a prophet in Exodus 15:20. Later, in Numbers 12, she spoke against her brother and was stricken with leprosy. She recovered but faded from the biblical record until her death was mentioned in Numbers 20:1.

Moses. The towering Moses was ancient Israel's great leader, lawgiver, priest, judge, shepherd, and prophet (Deuteronomy 34:10). Hosea said about Moses, "The Lord used a prophet to bring Israel up from Egypt" (Hosea 12:13). Despite his flaws, Moses served to point to a greater prophet yet to come (Deuteronomy 18:15–18)—Jesus Christ.

Nahum. Little is known about the author of the brief writing that bears the name Nahum. Based on his literate writing style, he seems to have been from a well-to-do family. He had a high view of God and His Word, and he condemned the Assyrians for their brazen idolatry, immorality, injustice, and all manner of sin.

Nathan. Nathan was the prophet who bravely confronted King David following his illicit affair with Bathsheba and the murder of her husband, Uriah (2 Samuel 11–12). Nathan accurately foretold the tragedy that would come from David's sin (2 Samuel 12:10–14).

Noah. The builder of the famous ark is often regarded as a prophet because God revealed to him things to come, and Noah's subsequent words and actions announced these certainties to a watching world (Genesis 6–9; see also Genesis 7:1; 2 Peter 2:5).

Obadiah. An obscure minor prophet, Obadiah gives us no family connections or hometown mentions. Even his name (meaning "worshiper of the Lord") was common; at least a dozen Old Testament men are named Obadiah. His book is the shortest writing in the Old Testament. Its two-part message? God sees and punishes sin, and God forgives and delivers sinners.

Oded. Oded was a little-known prophet who confronted the armies of the northern kingdom of Israel following their victory over Ahaz's forces from the southern kingdom of Judah. Oded warned of dire divine retribution if they mistreated their brothers and sisters from the south (2 Chronicles 28:1–15).

Samuel. The son of Elkanah and his wife Hannah, Samuel is regarded as the last of Israel's judges. After growing up under the tutelage of Eli the priest, "all Israel from Dan to Beersheba recognized that Samuel was attested as a prophet of the LORD" (1 Samuel 3:20). He anointed both Saul and David, the first two kings of Israel.

Shemaiah. A prophet during King Rehoboam's reign (930–913 BC), Shemaiah warned the king not to battle the ten tribes of the northern kingdom of Israel (1 Kings 12:22–24). He later chronicled Rehoboam's life (2 Chronicles 12:15), a writing that has disappeared from history.

Simeon. A devout old man in Jerusalem, Simeon is never called a prophet; but he was told by the "Holy Spirit that he would not die before he had seen the Lord's Messiah" (Luke 2:26). When Mary and Joseph brought the infant Jesus to the temple to dedicate Him to God, Simeon burst into a kind of prophecy about how this child would be "a light for revelation to the Gentiles, and the glory of . . . Israel" (Luke 2:32).

Simeon Niger. He is mentioned in Luke's list of prophets and teachers who were based in the Antioch church (Acts 13:1).

Uriah. A little-known figure during the time of King Jehoiakim, Uriah was the son of Shemaiah from Kiriath Jearim (Jeremiah 26:20). His prophetic messages echoed those of Jeremiah and enraged the king. Realizing his life was in danger, Uriah fled to Egypt. Jehoiakim sent men to find him and bring him back. When they did, "King Jehoiakim . . . had him struck down with a sword" (Jeremiah 26:23).

Zechariah. At least thirty people mentioned in the Bible shared the name Zechariah, which means "the Lord remembers." The prophet and author of the book Zechariah, however, is identified as the son of Berekiah and grandson of Iddo (Zechariah 1:1). He was born during Judah's Babylonian captivity. He returned to Jerusalem with the group of exiles led by Zerubbabel and became a priest. As both prophet and priest, Zechariah reminded his people of God's faithfulness in order to give them hope for the future.

Zephaniah. Zephaniah traced his lineage four generations back to Hezekiah (Zephaniah 1:1). A number of Jewish and Christian commentators have identified this Hezekiah with the king by the same name, but not all agree. The occasion for Zephaniah's prophecy was the deplorable spiritual and moral condition of Judah in the early days of Josiah's reign.

The Bible also tells about a number of false prophets:

* Ahab and Zedekiah (Jeremiah 29:21)
* Elymas, or Bar-Jesus (Acts 13:6–12)
* Hananiah (Jeremiah 28:5)
* Jezebel (Revelation 2:20; not to be confused with the Jezebel of the Old Testament)
* The false prophet of the book of Revelation (Revelation 16:13; 19:20; 20:10)
* The prophets of Baal who battled Elijah on Mount Carmel (1 Kings 18:13–40)
* Noadiah (Nehemiah 6:14)
* Simon the sorcerer (Acts 8:9–24)

Art Credits

1: Pavel Chagochkin/Shutterstock

2: Osugi /Shutterstock

3: Renata Sedmakova/Shutterstock

4: Anthony Correia/Shutterstock

5: Nicku/Shutterstock

7: Michael Candelori/Shutterstock

8: New York World-Telegram and the Sun staff photographer: Albertin, Walter, photographer./Wikimedia

9: Zvonimir Atletic/Shutterstock

10: Gary Yim/Shutterstock

11: Everett - Art/Shutterstock

12: Nicku/Shutterstock

13: Haslam Photography/Shutterstock

14: Unknown/Wikimedia

14: Renata Sedmakova/Shutterstock

14: Renata Sedmakova/Shutterstock

14: Renata Sedmakova/Shutterstock

14: Renata Sedmakova/Shutterstock

14: Renata Sedmakova/Shutterstock

14: Renata Sedmakova/Shutterstock

14: Zvonimir Atletic/Shutterstock

15: Anonymous/Wikimedia

15: Jojojoe/Wikimedia

15: Renata Sedmakova/Shutterstock

15: Renata Sedmakova/Shutterstock

15: Renata Sedmakova/Shutterstock

15: Zvonimir Atletic/Shutterstock

15: Zvonimir Atletic/Shutterstock

15: Zvonimir Atletic/Shutterstock

17: jorisvo/Shutterstock

18: Everett - Art/Shutterstock

19: Zvonimir Atletic/Shutterstock

21: PRESSLAB/Shutterstock

23: Everett Historical/Shutterstock

24: Truba7113/Shutterstock

26: Alexandros Michailidis/Shutterstock

28: pointbreak/Shutterstock

31: JekLi/Shutterstock

33: Internet Archive Book Images/ Wikimedia

34: Renata Sedmakova/Shutterstock

37: NesterovIV/Shutterstock

39: Arkady Mazor/Shutterstock

40: Krikkiat/Shutterstock

42: EQRoy/Shutterstock

43: ruskpp/Shutterstock

44: Triff/Shutterstock

46: jorisvo /Shutterstock

48: Zvonimir Atletic/Shutterstock

50: Lukas Plewnia/Wikimedia

52: Kelvin Helen Haboski/Shutterstock

55: ER_09/Shutterstock

56: Dennis Schugk/Wikimedia

58: Wellcome Library, London/Wikimedia

60: Andrey Mironov/Wikimedia

62: Illustrators of the 1897 Bible Pictures and What They Teach Us/Wikimedia

63: Berthold Werner/Wikimedia

64: Mikhail Markovskiy/Shutterstock

65: Diego Fiore/Shutterstock

67: FCerez/Shutterstock

68: sculpies/Shutterstock

71: Tate Britain/Wikimedia

72: Unknown/Wikimedia

74: Wellcome Library, London/Wikimedia

76: Jastrow/Wikimedia

78: dynamosquito/Wikimedia

80: Everett Historical/Shutterstock

81: Bogdan Ionescu/Shutterstock

82: Georgios Kollidas/Shutterstock

83: jorisvo/Shutterstock

84: Digitaler Lumpensammler/Wikimedia

86: fivespots/Shutterstock

87: Everett - Art/Shutterstock

88: Unknown/Wikimedia

89: The Yorck Project/Wikimedia

91: Zvonimir Atletic/Shutterstock

92: The Yorck Project/Wikimedia

94: Nicku/Shutterstock

95: Adam Jan Figel/Shutterstock

96: Ryan Rodrick Beiler/Shutterstock

100: Unknown/Wikimedia

103: Alex Earll/Shutterstock

104: Alafoto/Wikimedia

106: Yaffa/Wikimedia

107: Daimond Shutter/Shutterstock

108: Zvonimir Atletic/Shutterstock

109: Ailsa Mellon Bruce Fund/Wikimedia

110: fotorince/Shutterstock

113: Complete Works of Contemporary Art in Japan 7 Shigeru Aoki, Takeji Fujishima Shueisha, 1972/Wikimedia

114: Leon Skinner/Shutterstock

115: BMJ/Shutterstock

117: William Blake/Wikimedia

118: The National Gallery, UK/Wikimedia

121: Doré's English Bible/Wikimedia

122: William Blake/Wikimedia

123: Andre Marais/Shutterstock

124: Kevin Standage/Shutterstock

125: jorisvo/Shutterstock

126: Richard Mortel/Wikimedia

129: Oleg Ivanov IL/Shutterstock

130: Zvonimir Atletic/Shutterstock

131: Blake Archive / Tate Britain/ Wikimedia

132: Yelkrokoyade/Wikimedia

134: mikhail/Shutterstock

135: Alexander Gatsenko/Shutterstock

136: Currier & Ives/Wikimedia

137: CURAphotography/Shutterstock

139: José Luiz Bernardes Ribeiro/ Wikimedia

140: Renata Sedmakova/Shutterstock

143: Renata Sedmakova/Shutterstock

144: Renata Sedmakova/Shutterstock

146: Paul Brady Photography/ Shutterstock

148: Oleg Golovnev/Shutterstock

149: Google Art Project/Wikimedia

150: Nicku/Shutterstock

152: life_in_a_pixel/Shutterstock

154: IOSIF CHEZAN/Shutterstock

155: Renata Sedmakova/Shutterstock

156: Library of Congress, USA/Wikimedia

161: Piu_Piu/Shutterstock

162: Renata Sedmakova/Shutterstock

163: iman satria/Shutterstock

164: M0tty/Wikimedia

166: alefbet/Shutterstock

167: Julie Marshall/Shutterstock

168: Freedom Studio/Shutterstock

169: Renata Sedmakova/Shutterstock

170: Morphart Creation/Shutterstock

173: Renata Sedmakova/Shutterstock

174: AM113/Shutterstock

176: Christopher Slesarchik/Shutterstock

177: Renata Sedmakova/Shutterstock

179: AwOiSoAk KaOsIoWa/Wikimedia

180: zebra0209/Shutterstock

181: Riccardo Mayer/Shutterstock

183: Max Zalevsky/Shutterstock

184: Eduard Cebria/Shutterstock

185: Renata Sedmakova/Shutterstock

186: vkilikov/Shutterstock

187: Government Press Office (GPO), Israel/Wikimedia

188: Sarit Richerson/Shutterstock

191: Thomas Shahan/Wikimedia

192: Everett Historical/Shutterstock

194: John Theodor/Shutterstock

196: Everett - Art/Shutterstock

198: OPIS Zagreb/Shutterstock

200: arka38/Shutterstock

202: Rodsan18/Wikimedia

203: Renata Sedmakova/Shutterstock

205: nito/Shutterstock

207: Renata Sedmakova/Shutterstock

209: Bugra Berkin Birse/Shutterstock

210: Uoaei1/Wikimedia

212: Sascha Burkard/Shutterstock

214: HitManSnr/Shutterstock

216: Nagel Photography/Shutterstock

218: Ellen G. White Estate/Wikimedia

220: Hadrian/Shutterstock

222: Phillip Medhurst/Wikimedia

224: Adam Jan Figel/Shutterstock

227: Jose Carlos Alexandre/Shutterstock

228: John D Sirlin/Shutterstock

230: Phillip Medhurst/Wikimedia

233: jorisvo/Shutterstock

234: Milosh Mkv/Shutterstock

236: Phillip Medhurst/Wikimedia

238: Phillip Medhurst/Wikimedia

240: rocco constantino/Shutterstock

243: United States Department of Defense/Wikimedia

244: IM_photo/Shutterstock

249: WDnet Creation/Shutterstock

251: Zvonimir Atletic/Shutterstock

252: The William Blake Archive/Wikimedia

254: Zvonimir Atletic/Shutterstock

257: Leonard Zhukovsky/Shutterstock

258: No-Te Eksarunchai/Shutterstock

260: jorisvo/Shutterstock

262: Renata Sedmakova/Shutterstock

266: Renata Sedmakova/Shutterstock

267: Zvonimir Atletic/Shutterstock

268: Anonymous/Wikimedia

268: Jojojoe/Wikimedia

268: Zvonimir Atletic/Shutterstock

269: Renata Sedmakova/Shutterstock

269: Zvonimir Atletic/Shutterstock

270: Renata Sedmakova/Shutterstock

270: Zvonimir Atletic/Shutterstock

271: Renata Sedmakova/Shutterstock

271: Renata Sedmakova/Shutterstock

272: Renata Sedmakova/Shutterstock

272: Renata Sedmakova/Shutterstock

273: Unknown/Wikimedia

274: Renata Sedmakova/Shutterstock

275: Renata Sedmakova/Shutterstock